Anxiety:
A HEALING JOURNEY

Robin Sorenson

WESTBOW
PRESS
A DIVISION OF THOMAS NELSON

For Laina, Cam and Curtis

Love for you inspires.

Contents

Acknowledgments

Thank you to my good friends who gave much appreciated and valued editing advice along the way: Verna, Judy, Dorothy and Rosemary.

To Leon, who I love more than I can say, heartfelt thanks for your support through my journey, and your encouragement and suggestions for how to communicate it in written word.

About the Book

Though the examples of women suffering from anxiety in this book tell of real situations and thought patterns, each of the women is a composite of many women so that no one person can be recognized. If any of the examples of women in this book seem recognizable to you, it is because anxiety brings us all to many common experiences. That is why we benefit from spending time together. We find ourselves among people who genuinely relate to us. So enjoy the composite examples as a reminder that you are not alone on this journey.

PART ONE

In the Grip of Anxiety

CHAPTER ONE

Experiencing Brokenness

THINGS BEGAN FOR ME in such a vague, indiscernible way. Almost without thought or interest, I noticed that sometimes when I talked about things that really mattered to me, I would be out of breath. I was exhausted most of the time, but it didn't seem like I was that busy, even though my loved ones regularly expressed concern about my schedule.

Sure, things bothered me enough to keep me awake at night, but given how important the issues I wrestled with were, though I should have been sleeping, how could I? I didn't just care about things; I felt a need to solve them, work through all the possible scenarios of solving them, and consider all the "enemies" to the solution, and so I spent a lot of nights without much rest.

My hurried pace in life was necessary to deal with all the things that had plagued my mind in the night. My defense to my family's concern was that these things had to get done and get done properly. I had no choice. But many times in the middle of dealing with these life issues that I believed were so important, I'd lose my breath, breathing hard to finish a sentence as my cheeks grew hot.

I was totally perplexed when an overwhelming feeling of nausea and indigestion wracked my body. It would happen at the worst times, when we needed to be somewhere or when we had company over, and I would end up sitting in the bathroom wondering if my entire stomach was turning inside out. This same awful feeling sometimes came in the night, just as I was ready to drop into bed exhausted from the day, but because it happened so irregularly, I just wrote it off as too much rich food. But when it would once again sneak up on me, I found myself pondering this strange and aggressive indigestion that came and went within hours, leaving me exhausted and food shy for a day.

Then there was the lightheadedness and heart pounding that demanded I sit, better yet, lie down. I felt sure I was about to pass out. This made me feel panicky because I didn't understand what was happening to my body, and it seemed very likely to me that I was in some severe physical distress that needed immediate attention. Sometimes it was hard to swallow, and sometimes I felt tightness in my chest. Sometimes my lips felt numb or my tongue felt swollen. Thoughts of terminal illness always seemed to flit through my mind, as if every physical problem could have no simple explanation. But a breath of fresh air outside often helped, and because these awful symptoms did subside, I would settle down and carry on, weirdly lacking in curiosity about what had just happened to me. These feelings had been so long a part of my life, however intermittent, that I accepted them as normal.

Though I was home with two small children who kept me busy, the phone often rang with requests for my time. "Robin, we really need your help" were the words I didn't mind hearing at all. And I never said no. My calendar looked like a bistro's chalkboard menu, every possible space filled with writing. No moment was left unaccounted for as I worked in or led five different volunteer activities. Ironically, one of those was a lay-counseling ministry. I look back with awe at how, in the midst of my desire to help people, I was blind to the fact that I was in much need of help myself.

My life was characterized by anxious questions that ranged from trivial to important, but all weighed on me as if they were of vital importance. "What if I don't get where I'm going in time to sit with the people I want to be with?" "What if someone else gets the parking spot I want?" "What if an important decision gets made before I can weigh in on it?" "What if the teacher doesn't treat my child fairly?" "What if this ministry fails because I didn't hold it together?" "What if the sky falls because I'm not there to hold it up?" All of this often left me with a rock in the pit of my stomach because the responsibility was so great. I denied that my feelings of responsibility had anything to do with the awful physical symptoms that would periodically befall me.

Eventually, the time of questioning these terrible feelings became unavoidable as they began to increase in frequency and intensity that bleak January. I had just been diagnosed with a sinus infection. I was feeling completely overwhelmed by my responsibilities as a mother and volunteer. Then my son got a very bad case of croup that meant several sleepless nights, running him to the shower or letting freezing air in from the window when his breathing became badly labored. Exhausted, I then watched my husband a few days later get sicker than I'd ever known him to be. Two more sleepless nights, and we found out he had strep. And then February brought a pregnancy scare, which I responded to with utter despair at the thought of one more large responsibility.

By March I was a physical wreck. My sinus infection resisted every antibiotic I took, and I felt flu-like symptoms regularly. By the end of the month, I was not sleeping well, and by April, I was repeatedly awakened by nausea in the night. I stopped eating, believing I must have the stomach flu, but the nausea only intensified. Amazed at the power of this sinus infection, I dragged myself back to the doctor who gave me a new and more powerful antibiotic.

That night as I sat in our family room, I could feel that familiar old chill enter my body. The sensation was like a vial of chemicals suddenly released into my system causing my heart to pound, my entire digestive system to reel, and overwhelming heat to climb from my chest into my face. The sense of fear was overpowering. I was sure I must've been having a heart attack; or was it a reaction to the new antibiotics? Whatever it was, I felt sure it was life-threatening. And so the argument in my head started, the rational woman pitted against the anxious woman who feared that every illness was terminal.

> *"But just a minute here, Robin. You've felt this way before and you didn't die."*
>
> "Maybe, but this time I'm taking new medication and I could easily be having an allergic reaction."
>
> *"You've never had an allergic reaction before. Why would you start now?"*
>
> "It's a well-known fact that allergies can start at any point, even if you've never reacted before. I'm not going to ignore this and die!"

And so goes the ongoing internal argument. Brief moments of rational thought mingled with much greater moments of abject fear, fear winning in the end.

That night I went to bed and never slept. The next night I went to bed exhausted and hoped desperately for sleep, but finally woke my husband, Leon, at 3:00 a.m. I knew I was on the verge of dying, and for the second night in a row I hadn't slept at all, not even briefly. Every time I'd begin to drift off, something would jar me awake. My teeth chattered as my entire body shook uncontrollably. I felt like I was going to jump out of my skin and I knew I needed to go to the emergency room. Once there, I was so weak that they got me a wheelchair. My hands and arms tingled, and I knew I was on the verge of passing out when they took me to my cubicle. Interestingly, once the doctor came in all these terrible feelings began to disappear. He handed me a sedative and told me to go off the antibiotics, though he didn't like the idea because they were starting to work. I could tell he didn't think the antibiotic was the culprit, and I was curious about why he thought I needed a sedative. Leon wondered out loud how I suddenly became better once the doctor checked me out. I didn't admit it, but I wondered too.

I took the sedative, which was another anxiety-inducing event, but surprisingly it helped and I slept that night. Then I slept the next night and the next with no sedative. This confirmed for me that I had been right to believe the antibiotics were the problem. Unfortunately, though confident in my assessment, the feelings returned a few nights later and recurred for several nights in a row. By this time, I was sure a doctor would think I was crazy and I had a pretty good suspicion Leon thought there wasn't really anything wrong with me, but it was impossible for anyone to understand the desperation I felt. I was so sick that my powers of concentration had left me, and I felt utterly helpless to understand even *what* I was feeling, let alone *why*. Night after night I was plagued, shivering with a familiar fear I'd felt many times in my life, when my imaginings turned to intense worrying. But this time there was nothing to be worried about. I felt no sense of danger to anyone. Why couldn't I stop this?

During the day, I was so weak and incapable of any decision making that I couldn't even face getting my six-year-old daughter up and ready for school. Leon had to leave late for work so that he could take care of what I simply could not do. All I was able to do was lie on the couch in a constant state of strange terror that seemed to manifest itself physically in ways that rendered me incapable of normal daily functioning. My family did all they could to be supportive and understanding, but I felt all alone, as if an invisible wall separated me from their world. I would look at people going about their daily lives and marvel at how they could be so oblivious to the fact that the world was such a terrifying place to be. I couldn't imagine how anyone could muster up the energy to laugh. It all eluded me in this dark tunnel of isolating fear. This powerful sinus infection theory seemed suddenly very inadequate, and I decided to head back to my doctor.

My condition, badly deteriorated by a sinus infection and nights of sleeplessness, might have caused me to be an enigma to many doctors, but as I told my doctor about my nights and the feelings of terror, she said with a confidence I'll never forget, "I know what is wrong with you. You have anxiety disorder." She proceeded to explain anxiety disorder to me and tell me about the treatments available. At this point, I guess I should have been thrilled to have my problem figured out, but I wasn't. I started to cry as she described my illness and I cried all the way down the elevator to the pharmacy, crying harder still as I handed the prescription to the pharmacist. The pharmacist kindly looked at me and said, "You know this is just a chemical replacement, don't you?" Was she *nuts*? Didn't she understand I'd just been handed a life sentence called WEAKNESS? As desperately as I wanted relief, I did not want to be going through what I knew people had always referred to as a "nervous breakdown." I knew I could read about myself in psychological diagnostic books and journals. I knew my social work colleagues would have treated patients like me, and that knowledge brought even deeper shame. This was the ultimate failure with a capital "F".

Medications had to be slightly altered in the next little while. Unfortunately, the anti-depressant that was making me better started to increase my jumpiness, so my doctor worked on adjustments until I started to feel better. Though the medications finally did work, I still had some difficult experiences while they were sorted out. For the first two days of the changed medications, I experienced a horrifying thing—flat affect. I'd observed people with this problem in my work as a social worker, but I never understood it until it happened to me. I felt nothing: no happiness, no anxiety, just absolute nothingness. I could finally experience rest, but there was no satisfaction in this void of emotion. It was as if I didn't even exist. These days were the deepest and darkest I'd ever known. I had reached such a low emotional point that I had no answers left inside of me and I recognized that I had lost all power to help myself. My doctor's answers were my last hope and so I listened with complete compliance.

Once the anti-depressants began to take effect in the next four weeks, I regained an appetite. Soon, I could start participating in family conversations and even the occasional event. My husband had a work banquet in a city close by and I decided to go with him. I managed to attend the banquet, but my head pounded with what had become a regular tension headache, and I could only manage to chat for so long before anxiety threatened to creep back in. I could do nothing that held any amount of excitement or stress. With an exaggerated and foolish sense of responsibility, I resumed some of my volunteer work, but realize now I had nothing to offer at that point and would have served everyone better if I'd stayed home. I felt, and was, for the first time in my life, frail and incapable of coping with normal life. I couldn't even watch television because the fast-paced commercials during my kid's programs intensified my state of anxiety. I lived walking on eggshells, careful of every move in case something triggered what was now a terrifying state of mind that my brain chose for itself, quite apart from my will. No amount of calm thinking or sane reasoning worked. I was totally at the mercy of what my mind was doing, and I felt trapped and very much alone.

As I walked through those four weeks before the antidepressants took full effect, my experience was similar to being lowered into a tank with a slow stream of anxiety trickling in. If a cup of herbal tea or some soothing music could divert my attention, the anxiety would stop and I'd emerge from the tank. But if I was unsuccessful, I'd stay in that tank and the anxiety would start gushing in: reaching my waist, chest and soon over my head. No diversion could pull me out once I'd reached that point.

The sense of impending doom and the absolute panic associated with this was, and still is, impossible to describe. I've always been a proponent of "pulling yourself up by your boot straps", but I just could not do it. I'd tell myself this was ridiculous; there was no need to feel this way. But my mind seemed to be beyond reasoning with. It was in charge and I no longer had any say. Wherever it chose to take me, I was forced to go. It's a terrible thing to be held captive by your own mind. I was broken, wondering if my life had been shattered into many different pieces that I'd never pick up again.

The self-sufficient, competent woman who I had once known myself to be had vanished into thin air. One thing I clung to, fogged as my judgment was at the time: this state couldn't be something I must live with forever. I had a sense that there was something in me that had brought this about, something very much hidden from my sight, and I cried out to God to reveal it to me. Brokenness humbled me.

CHAPTER TWO

The House Where Anxiety Lives

ANXIETY IS EXTREMELY DEMANDING of us. I know of no one who can just ignore it. The profound distress of anxiety will often lead people to seek treatment to alleviate it. But what is anxiety and how does it work? These were two important questions for me as I began to recover from my "crash", and I wrestled with these puzzling things in prayer. The conclusion I have eventually come to is that there are two vital things within anxiety which must be addressed: the symptom and the underlying problem.

Anxiety, though it masquerades very convincingly as the problem, is only the symptom. Of course, anxiety begins to create problems of its own when it interferes with our ability to deal with life, but when looking at ways to effectively deal with anxiety, it is important to recognize it for what it really is, and that is a symptom. This is important because it is easy to fall into a belief that anxiety is just a part of who we are, a genetic wiring which is ours to bear for a lifetime. But if we understand it as the symptom of something else, we can go on to address what it is pointing to.

Mark Twain said, "I've had a lot of worries in my life, most of which never happened." Can you relate to this? I sure can. As a young adult, I believed many of my physical illnesses to be potentially life-threatening. In my early career I worked as a social worker in the hospital and I experienced left arm and chest pain when I was on the heart unit, and headaches and leg weakness when I was on the neurological unit. I'd had cancer, multiple sclerosis and heart disease so many times—why, I was a walking miracle! Irrational and excessive fear for my health had always been a significant part of my life, but I thought this was normal.

When my daughter was born and I suddenly had someone extremely precious to be responsible for, fear and worry naturally increased for me. Almost three years later my son was born which doubled what was precious to us, doubling also my opportunity for worry. Of course, as with any child, there were times of concern, but I would experience concern even when it wasn't warranted. It got to the point that their cough or fever induced panic and anxiety in me.

Panic happens when we perceive a threat. It activates in our bodies what has become known as the "fight/flight" response. The body's protective chemicals are released, providing us with a hyper-alertness in preparation for fight or flight from a threatening situation. It's designed to protect us from harm or death. This response is appropriate if your child is attacked by a bear or you need to defend yourself from an assailant. It does little good when we are ruminating, worrying, or mulling over a frustration or potential crisis, yet these same physiological responses occur. How deadly is a child's fever, a news report about the latest super-germ, a looming deadline, or a slow-moving vehicle making you late for an appointment? We don't require all the energy these chemicals are giving us to fight an assailant, or pick up our child and run from a bear. So there we sit, in this stew of chemicals our body doesn't need, and before we know it, we're having a panic attack.

Over the years, as my body was regularly put in this "fight/flight" response because of my regular state of worry, I slowly and unwittingly eroded my mental health. When I got sick with anxiety disorder, it felt as if my body had grown so accustomed to panic that my brain got locked in like car tires in deep ruts on a dirt road. With fear and worry, I had so often induced this response that my brain just seemed to have found itself stuck in panic mode.

After some time, I could look back and see how chronic worry had escalated into my inability to turn off the panic signal, regardless of how calm my circumstances. This was an important beginning for me as I took my eyes off of my anxiety as the culprit. Rather than a disease wired into my DNA, a problem that would assail me on and off for the rest of my life, I now saw anxiety was pointing me to something other than itself and I needed to pay attention.

Imagine a doctor examining a child with a very high fever that has persisted for a week. Were that doctor to suggest only continued acetaminophen use, and send the child and parent home with no further investigation, we would be suspicious. Fevers are only symptoms of a problem, and their persistence and recurrence indicates something deeper is going on. The fever does make the child extremely uncomfortable, and the doctor is right to prescribe a solution to that discomfort. But the story can't end there. In the same way, anxiety is extremely uncomfortable, and we need to address it with something. But dealing only with a symptom ignores the underlying problem that brings that symptom back time and time again.

Once I was diagnosed by my doctor and she prescribed medication that did in fact work, I experienced incredible relief as the anxiety gradually subsided more and more over the next several months. But we would have made a mistake if we had dealt only with the symptom and were content to leave it at that. This incredible gift of relief that the medications provide can lull a person into believing that the problem has been dealt with. Some people who suffer with anxiety are resigned to a lifetime of medication, believing that this is just a part of their life that they need to accept. But I believe we've only just begun at this point. We have to be wary of becoming fixated on the symptom when it is only pointing us to the real problem.

Before we move on to the problem itself, it is important to realize that we're not in a position to deal with this problem alone. Anxiety can become a medical issue related to how the chemicals in the brain are working. Doctors are the qualified go-to people for this. You won't be in a position to decide if this is the case or not, so when struggling with anxiety, it is always a must to see your doctor.

I have mentored women over the past decade who have asked for help only after they feel anxiety has made a train wreck of their lives. Rarely have I met an anxious person who recognizes their problem early and decides to "nip it in the bud." Rather, anxious people, and I've met dozens, tend not to see anxiety as a problem they have. They don't recognize, as I didn't, that they have inordinate and unreasonable amounts of fear and worry in their lives. If they do recognize this, they see their anxiety as a reasonable response to their life problems. It often takes a major crisis of anxiety for a person to accept that they are getting into trouble and need help.

By the time crisis has motivated a person, it is highly likely a doctor will prescribe medication. This, put in its simplest form, has to do with neurotransmitters that have stopped properly doing their job in our brains. Medications were designed to deal with this problem and get the brain back to its normal function. For some reason, which I do not wholly understand, anxious people, and in particular anxious people of faith, distrust medications to treat things going on in the brain. It is as if the brain were not an organ of the body, but something entirely outside the realm of the physical and, therefore, off-limits to medicine and a doctor's recommendations. We need to address anxiety as a medical issue once it begins to impair normal functioning because often there is a legitimate chemical malfunction in our brain's system. Medication helps to get things back on track.

My doctor said I needed to take an anti-depressant, and potentially a sedative, to get me through the particularly tough anxiety attacks. I put them in my mouth and had someone I love close by to hold my hand, while I considered all the terrible possibilities. The doctor may reassure you that your throat won't close up, that you won't go into a coma, and that your heart won't stop. I wasn't convinced so I held someone's hand. The doctor may reassure you that you won't become addicted to anti-depressants, but I wasn't convinced. Luckily, I realized that the internet was not my best friend. I could easily have gotten myself lost in the worry about facts and figures that I wasn't qualified to assess wisely.

Thankfully, I just listened to my doctor. If your doctor prescribes a sedative to take until the anti-depressants begin working, which could take weeks, she'll also tell you sedatives have addictive qualities. She'll likely also explain that you won't become addicted because you're too terrified of addiction to take them, more terrified than the terror of the anxiety that is currently engulfing you. My doctor's question to me was, "In the last week Robin, how many times did you need the sedative, but refused to take it?" It was an excellent question because I'd taken it only once when I would have been greatly helped about five other times. All I could think about was the possibility of addiction, a possibility that couldn't have been further off given my extreme displeasure and resistance to taking medication. I would have served myself better taking the few that I needed during that short time. After all of this internal struggle about taking medication, just as the doctor had told me, it began to work after a few weeks. This was an incredibly welcome relief.

Medication is not our only course of symptom relief. There are a number of others, though they definitely will be less effective and potentially only mildly helpful once we've reached the point where the doctor is recommending anti-depressants. There are some important things we can do, though. These include exercise, caffeine reduction, healthy food choices, relaxation techniques like listening to soft music, meditation on scripture, locking the bathroom door and taking a restful hot bath, and getting adequate amounts of sleep (don't fool yourself into believing you are just one of those people who only needs five hours a night; five hours likely means your sleep is disrupted). Of all these, exercise is the most immediate and effective. Endorphins released by brisk exercise do a great deal of good, though they won't completely solve the problem. Of course, this exercise must only be started on the advice of your doctor. No matter how you cut it, your doctor plays a primary role on your journey.

While the techniques listed above are helpful, they are not the only answer and anxiety often persists when people opt to avoid medication all together. Medicine and natural techniques are helpful and under the watchful eye of a good physician, medication does not condemn us to a life of sedative and anti-depressant use. But both of these are only the "fever" relief until the underlying problem is addressed and resolved. A gauge of whether your doctor has a good grasp on the problem and treatment of anxiety is if they prescribe medications along with insisting that you must deal with the underlying issues. Anxiety, though it may have a genetic predisposition, also largely stems from how we have learned to think about and deal with life. Whether anxiety is a result of genetics, learning, or both, we are not left with hopelessness for healing, but more about that later.

My doctor didn't mince words. She told me the symptom and the underlying problems must be addressed at the same time if I wished to find myself effectively dealing with anxiety. If you're like me, your back will arch, your pride will be wounded, and you'll likely resist the idea something is wrong with the way you think. Yet I now firmly believe our thoughts and beliefs are responsible for our feelings of anxiety. Anxiety is simply an emotion we experience as a result of these thoughts. It's a complex emotion that isn't fully explained by the words fear or worry. It has its own feelings that manifest themselves physically as they are compounded by chemicals telling our bodies to do all manner of things. Yet it remains an emotion, a feeling or feelings driven by something else.

Emotional Signs and Symptoms	Physical Signs and Symptoms
irritability	pounding heart
restlessness	numbness or tingling
feelings of dread	nausea
jumpiness/easily startled	abdominal discomfort
overwhelmed	chattering teeth
anticipation of danger	dizziness/fainting
fear of imminent death	choking/breathlessness
chronic worry	poor immunity
anger	fatigue
disorganization/forgetfulness	disturbed sleep
poor concentration	tension headaches
fear/avoidance of certain social situations	frequent doctor visits for various ailments

Unlike thoughts and beliefs, emotions are morally neutral; they may not feel good, but this doesn't make them wrong. To focus on the emotion/emotions we call anxiety, we are missing the mark by dealing with something that has no inherent value other than to express something else that is going on. So when we "feel" emotions, we need to understand what is happening somewhere else, or what they are indicating to us. That is why wise people in our lives tell us not to trust our emotions alone. It is precisely because emotions are indicative of something going on in our minds, but they are not the "what" that is going on. The "what" is our thoughts and beliefs, the things we cling to as unalterable truth about us and our world.

Jesus told a parable:

> "When an evil spirit comes out of a man, it goes through arid places seeking rest and does not find it. Then it says, "I will return to the house I left." When it arrives, it finds the house swept clean and put in order. Then it goes and takes seven other spirits more wicked than itself, and they go in and live there. And the final condition of that man is worse than the first."[1]

An important truth about the mind exists here. When we sweep our mind "clean" of symptoms of anxiety (with medication, relaxation techniques, diet restrictions, etc.) we've ignored the "house" or mind that remains. Nothing about its structure has changed, so though it appears clean, it is only temporarily unoccupied. Unless the structure changes, the invitation for a return is open. If anxiety is the dust we sweep out the door, our thoughts and beliefs are the structure of the house that creates the conditions within which anxiety flourishes unchecked. If we only deal with the emotions (our anxiety), and neglect the structure (our thoughts and beliefs), those old emotions will flow back in, and this effect can be multiplied by how much failure and despair we feel because it returned. Before it returned, we may have thought with great relief, "Ah, it was only temporary", but on its return we now somehow feel anxiety is a part of us—maybe forever. And our condition is worse than the first as this new fear breeds more anxiety.

"Truths" we formulate give meaning to circumstances around us, which then cause us to react with certain emotions. The emotions don't cause themselves, but rise out of something we think or believe. The interesting thing about thoughts is that they are so complex and so deeply embedded we are often not even aware of them. In less than a second, our mind can give meaning to an event and elicit an emotion without our awareness of what the thought process was. These thoughts describe to us the meaning of the circumstances and what we must do in the midst of them. But we are hard-pressed to unravel these webs of complex thought. A revealed and challenged thought can be tested for accuracy and truth. Thoughts and beliefs buried by years of unawareness need to be brought to the surface for light to shine on them. So David wisely prayed, "Search me, O God, and know my heart; test me and know my anxious thoughts. See if there is any offensive way in me..."[2]

It's helpful to have examples of which thoughts and beliefs might lead to anxiety. One example is the belief that many anxious people hold about personal responsibility to fix problems, even anxiety itself. Beth is an excellent example of this. Beth suffered a very severe crisis with anxiety during the Christmas rush one year. She went to the doctor because her anxiety attacks were almost constant, and she had become unable to function because of them. She was in the middle of a very busy and demanding time, both at home and at church. She didn't want to risk disappointing her children or the many people at church who were counting on her to make Christmas celebrations happen, so she went for help even though it really didn't sit well to ask for it. Her doctor prescribed anti-depressants, and though immediately skeptical, she agreed to take them.

After a month, Beth began to feel better and so decided to wean herself off the pills. She believed the problem was fixed, partly because she got a boost from the pills, which she was convinced she only needed a few of, and mostly because she had cut back on her schedule and Christmas was now over. She saw herself as back to normal with no need for help from the medication. Because Beth felt responsible for solving this problem, she took over the responsibility of deciding what a sufficient amount of medication was and when it should be stopped, though she herself had no medical expertise.

Here's how she thought:

"I'm having overwhelming bouts of anxiety I can't seem to solve for myself and I haven't got the luxury of waiting for a solution—I guess I'll have to talk to the doctor—the doctor insists I need medications so I'll take them to buy me a bit of time to figure this out for myself— now that I've taken them for a short time I'm just fine—false alarm after all, just a busy time of year and a strange little blip in my response to it—I'm ready to get myself off these unnecessary medications."

A second example of the thought processes involved is what occurred once Beth had reduced the level of her medication. Almost inevitably, a relapse of symptoms came as the medications were rendered ineffective by the inadequate dosage. Her doctor gave the medicine he knew would be adequate, but Beth, without medical expertise of her own, decided she knew best. She had a relapse of her symptoms, only this time they were more intense. Having initially seen improvement as evidence she had won the battle with anxiety due to modifications to her lifestyle, she saw this relapse as a great failure on her part. Failure was unacceptable because she took responsibility for having the competency to fix the problem. My question to her was "Can you see where are you putting yourself between a 'rock and a hard place?'", because that is what I'd asked myself so many times.

This is an important question. We often place ourselves in the middle of two assumed possibilities, neither of which is possible. Anxious people tend to be strong-willed and tenacious, continually placing themselves between two impossibilities and then demanding they overcome them. This was true of Beth. In the first example, Beth demanded she be her own doctor for a problem that had up until now eluded her ability to solve. Being her own doctor was the "rock" because she was not qualified, and fixing the anxiety was the "hard place" because it had already proven itself to be outside of her control. These were the two impossible "possibilities" she expected to overcome. In the second example when she had a relapse of symptoms, they were even worse because now she was demanding that she fix something she thought she already had, and she was faced with terrible disappointment at her failure. As her unreasonable demands increased in intensity, her symptoms ramped up along with them. This is the "rock and the hard place" of putting yourself between two possibilities that never were possible.

This is well illustrated by the various decisions we often obsess over when we are ill enough with anxiety that we are desperate for help:

- "Will I tell my doctor what is going on?"
- "Will I fill the prescription I've been given?"
- "Will I take the pills now in my possession?"
- "Will I take the full dosage and for how long?"
- "When will I start weaning off the medications and by how much?"

Obsession best describes this process as we, armed with internet research and impaired by anxiety's constant drain on our mind's clarity, insist that we should be able to do that which is beyond our ability to do.

Imagine a different approach. Imagine that we accepted that we can't overcome our struggle with anxiety because it has persisted despite our best efforts. Now imagine that we decide to go to the doctor and trust her advice, regularly report back on our progress with the medication, and listen to what she tells us in a spirit of cooperation, allowing her medical expertise to solve any problems as they come up. Yes, I'm suggesting you relinquish control of fixing your anxiety to help you better cope with it by not fueling even greater anxiety. That is the whole idea behind the "rock and the hard place" concept. We have to learn to accept our limitations, rejecting our ridiculous and unattainable expectations if we are going to make a contribution to healthy thoughts that can replace the ones that spur anxiety on. We will talk about many more "rock and hard place" scenarios in later chapters.

Anxiety doesn't tell you what is wrong; it only signals that there is something wrong. But this signal is intense and painful so a caring doctor will help relieve the pain. Once that signal is no longer felt, it's easy to think the problem is solved, but the thing that is wrong still hasn't been addressed. That structure or "house" you've built over years of allowing unchallenged thoughts like "I must achieve the impossible" to run rampant and untested for accuracy is still standing, and so anxiety still has a home to return to. For this reason, taking medication alone will never be enough.

I'm making a claim that anxiety is not a genetic predisposition that will dog us for the rest of our lives (this claim is *not* referring to anxiety when it stems from a more serious mental health disorder that may involve psychosis, as an example). I live a different life than I used to and that is the basis for my claim. There has been a fundamental shift in how I approach what life brings and, as a consequence of that, I haven't since needed medication nor do I experience interference with my life on a regular basis from anxiety. I am not, however, claiming it is possible to live life in complete peace and calm, never again encumbered by any anxious feelings or even the occasional panic attack. I do know that what I've learned is how God can help me sanely navigate the problems, and even the storms, of life that once gripped me in paralyzing anxiety. I'm not suggesting you'll never feel anxiety again. What I am saying is that God provides a way to make it possible to live a life largely free of its paralysis, and he teaches us how to rest our anxiety in him whose peace transcends our ability to comprehend. His peace is a gift he wants to give us.

We are blessed, if that's possible to accept, to be overcome by anxiety, because it is at that point that we are most likely to allow God to show us the truth about our real problem. A leper can't feel pain, and so goes on to do much unintended harm to their body. Anxiety is our emotion that tells us we're in harm's way. If we only manage to suppress the feeling, we've ignored the real danger. These are the two fronts that anxiety faces us with: the emotions, also known as the symptom, and the problem itself. The problem has two layers. The first is the "house", our thoughts and beliefs we've discussed in this chapter. But the most crucial is the second layer, the foundation of our house, which is our identity.

Anxiety at a Glance

Structural Framework:

Identity

↓

Thoughts and Beliefs

↓

Symptom—Anxiety

CHAPTER THREE

Who Am I?

BEFORE WE GO ON to look, with concrete examples, at the thoughts that lead to our feelings of anxiety, there is one final layer to the problem which completes the outline of how anxiety works. I want to borrow another example from Jesus' brilliant imagery to explain. In Matthew 7, Jesus said we must build our house on a foundation of rock rather than sand, so when natural disaster comes, which it inevitably will, our house will not fall with a great crash. We who struggle with anxiety need to build our house of thoughts and beliefs on firm ground so that when the natural stresses of life occur, we don't get swept away in a state of crisis.

So then, what is that foundation? Jesus said the foundation is the truth of his words—God's word. That truth is what defines both him and us. He tells us who he is and who we are in relation to him. Our solid foundation is when we define ourselves as God has defined us, and when we define him as his words define him. Jesus used this illustration to explain to his religiously devout listeners that they had misconceptions about that foundation. They didn't intentionally deny God's truth and nor do we. When we find ourselves overwhelmed by anxiety because of disasters, real or imagined, it is ultimately an identity issue. Our foundation is shaky and unstable when our identities are different than those God intended for us, and this is the layer we need to understand if we are ever to deal with the surface issue of anxiety.

Our identities are to be God-given. He's our Creator and Definer. Yet we often try to attain our identity through our own competency and achievement. We also accept it from the wrong sources. We look to our families and friends, bosses and co-workers, for affirmation and definition. Both the attempt to attain identity for ourselves and to receive it from wrong sources creates an unstable identity because it is wholly dependent on human weakness and mortality. It's like a foundation of unstable sand.

My favorite, unfortunately out-of-print, devotional quotes a passage written by Emilie Griffin that points us to our stable foundation. She explains that it is God himself who gives us our definition. "It's an identity we can't discover for ourselves and that others can't discover in us—the mystery of who we really are." Rather than seek our identity out in the world, Griffin invites us to recognize that God is waiting to tell us who we are, but this can only happen when we abandon the restless pursuit of finding it for ourselves, instead waiting expectantly and patiently for that revelation to come from him.[3]

My own first encounter with God on the identity issue occurred shortly after being diagnosed with anxiety disorder. I was still reeling from the sense of utter failure that this diagnosis had meant to me, when I experienced a five-night sleepless streak because my anxiety just would not abate. Entirely overwhelmed with panic and terrible fatigue, I could only call out God's name. There are times in life when all we can ask is "help" because we can't find the energy or words to ask for more. This was where I found myself. One of those nights, while everyone else slept, I desperately cried out for help and I could hear, not audibly, but very clearly in my mind:

"Robin, all I need to do is breathe a whisper
on you and you will blow over like a blade
of grass."

It was unmistakable. Where moments earlier there had been fog, suddenly I had complete clarity. I knew the source of these words. I had cried out to God and finally, in my state of utter weakness with no distractions and defenses left, I was hearing his gentle chastisement. I was experiencing what Elijah experienced. God doesn't present himself in the wind, earthquake and fire. He speaks in a gentle whisper, and most of the time I'm not listening intently enough to hear it. But believe me, I was more than ready to listen and so listen I did.

His sentence repeated itself over and over in my head, and there was no anger or unkindness in it. In those words I felt an amazing tenderness and love for me. God simply wanted me to understand that yes, in fact, I was weak. The time for truth had finally arrived. God had decided it was time to free me from my delusion that I could be self-sufficient.

There I lay, cradled in the all-loving and all-knowing presence of my God, all pretenses laid bare, and yet he still loved me. When God is in the room with you, making himself known, you can't miss him. And so I listened, allowing his gentle chastisement to wash over me. With joy, I embraced this act of love. God would never lie to me, even to save my feelings. That night in that room was my worst and my greatest; God's love is often most evident in the darkest times of life when we've reached the end of ourselves. My current state revealed to me a truth about myself that I'd been too busy being competent to understand. There I was, stripped of all masks, a pauper. "Blessed are the poor in spirit"[4] suddenly made sense to me. For in this darkest hour I experienced the inexplicable joy of my own poverty. As Oswald Chambers wrote:

> "The bedrock in Jesus Christ's kingdom
> is poverty, not possession; not decisions
> for Jesus Christ, but a sense of absolute
> futility—I cannot begin to do it. Then
> Jesus says—Blessed are you."[5]

Blessed was I.

Prior to my dark descent into anxiety, I lacked personal insight. I looked at the surface of my life and what I found there was pretty comfortable. Certainly there was stress and strain, as with all lives, but I failed to see my contribution to this. I viewed any of my problems as existing outside of myself, struggles to be faced and dealt with as forces coming from without, placing undue pressure on me as I tried to deal with them. I was a busy mom who found time to be a busy Christian. I was staying home to raise my kids, volunteering at school, training and leading women in a lay-counseling ministry at my church, working on a steering committee with Social Services in my city to join efforts with city churches to meet the needs of the poor, and serving on the committee charged with the spiritual leadership of our church. This schedule seemed reasonable to me. I enjoyed all aspects of this work, passionate about everything I worked on. Obviously, these roles all came with enormous challenges because each one had a major significance of its own, not the least of which being the formative years for my children. Now I look at this list and rather than seeing an accomplished woman, I see an overwhelmed one about to butt up against her own humanity.

The roles in my life I had chosen to take on were the result of an enormous blind spot. I had a Self-sufficient identity that convinced me I was needed. I couldn't say no to good things because I believed I was responsible to make them happen. Though all these things exhausted me, and I sometimes panicked about not being able to hold it all together, I couldn't see that my belief in my indispensability was way off course and destructive. My value and worth was measured by how self-sufficient and competent I was. It gained me the approval of others, and I believed it gained me the approval of God. What I didn't understand, in the whirlwind of a life of good works, was that God was more than unimpressed. He was determined to rid me of my deluded and destructive theology.

That night when God spoke so clearly to me, he spoke directly out of Isaiah 40, though I didn't discover this until months later. Isaiah 40:6a-7 reads:

> "All men are like grass, and all their glory
> is like the flowers of the field. The grass
> withers and the flowers fall, because the

breath of the Lord blows on them. Surely
the people are grass."

This wonderful chapter in Isaiah goes on to describe the comforting truth that, though we are mortal and weak, God will never grow tired or weary, and he will increase the power of the weak when they *trust in him*. Total trust in God makes our weakness give way to his strength.

When I had reached the point of being so ill, it became abundantly clear to me that I had viewed myself as Self-sufficient. It wasn't just that I viewed this trait as valuable; I was in crisis when the doctor gave me my diagnosis because she wounded my identity of Self-sufficiency. Who I believed myself to be was at odds with the diagnosis. It was clear that I was not Self-sufficient, not who I'd believed myself to be. There was no doubt that I was now entirely weak, and not only in this particular moment, but also in the course of life, because I knew I couldn't control when anxiety might leave or return. Faced with my utter inability to control my illness stripped me of my identity and left me terrified. If I wasn't who I thought I was, then who was I?

God's gentle words to me out of Isaiah were my reminder of God's intended identity for me, that of complete dependence on him—weakness in my human frailty that was totally safe in the strength of God. The remedy wasn't to tell Robin how to fix this problem of weakness and get her act together. Though my first reaction to feeling weak was negative and defeatist, I came to realize that human weakness isn't a frailty to be solved, but a safe reality if God is who he says he is. Now the questions became apparent. Can I trust him? Do I believe he is who he says he is, and do I know who he says I am? If my foundation as Self-sufficient was profoundly challenged by this current reality in my life, who did I now define myself to be?

These questions aren't always obvious to us when we're dealing with intermittent or prolonged bouts of anxiety. Though we might know what large problem is troubling us, perhaps a looming deadline or a child struggling in school, we have neglected to examine the "house" of our thoughts and beliefs about that problem, let alone considering who we define ourselves to be within that house. I'll give three examples of everyday problems to explain what I mean.

There is a young girl in junior high school, who, confident she'll be chosen, tries out for her school play. She leaves the house the morning of the try-out excited and enthusiastic, but she comes home from school deflated. She tells her mom she is almost certain she didn't get the part because there were so many other more talented girls. That night, after tucking her daughter in after a long discussion about the disappointment, the mom goes to bed wide awake and feeling much anxiety for her daughter. Though it's obvious to this mom that she feels anxious and worried about her daughter, as she schemes about how to resolve this, she's unlikely to be aware of the thoughts and beliefs that instantly impact how she addresses the problem. These thoughts determine how we react, but are so deeply ingrained we're hardly aware they exist. Observe how these thoughts progress:

> "What if my daughter isn't good enough to be picked—she won't be in the play—I'll have a very disappointed child—disappointment like this will wound her—I am responsible for my child's protection from being wounded—I have to do whatever it takes to prevent this—I must rescue her."

Observe what this mom is thinking. Her belief system says disappointment is a terrible thing that must be avoided. But this belief is faulty because disappointment and learning how to handle it is a major source of our personal growth. Not only is it impossible to protect your children from disappointment, it is desirable for them to encounter it and receive coaching on how to handle it. But this mom isn't aware of her flawed thoughts, and so she can't correct them. Buried deeper still from her sight is the identity that has driven this thought process, and that is the identity of Rescuer. She defines herself as Rescuer for her daughter. It is her responsibility to rescue her daughter from disappointment in life, and so she will set out to plan and devise whatever she can to do this, otherwise her identity is at stake. Let's return to the two impossibilities of this situation. The "rock" is that she has no power over the decision about the play, and the "hard place" is that disappointment in life is inevitable.

Here is the second example. You have an important decision to make that will impact other people and so you apply a process to evaluate all the options in the decision. After careful consideration, you make the decision. You let people know what it is and someone angrily and inappropriately tells you it's the wrong one and that you would have done well to consult them first. They weren't in the process for reasons of conflict of interest, and still you find yourself anxious about what they've said to you. Perhaps this is your thought process:

> "Did I make a bad decision?—this is an area I didn't understand with complete expertise so I had to look carefully at every angle—maybe I've made a mistake—I didn't look hard enough for that "right answer"—not finding the "right answer" reveals weakness in my competency—I am to be perfectly competent in all things I do."

The thinking here is that perfect competence is achievable and evidenced by the ability to always find that one right answer. In fact, this isn't true. There are many good answers in life, as evidenced by the many different approaches people take. Creativity is limitless, and so are good answers that solve problems. There is no such thing as a perfect answer that will prevent all possible problems. The root cause of this thinking is that the person's identity is Perfectly Competent. It's obvious what the "rock and the hard place" are in this example. I must be perfectly competent (rock) or I will not find the one right answer (hard place).

One final example is a grown woman who lives close to her mother. The woman's husband has just received a job opportunity that he's been wanting for many years, but it requires a move to another part of the country. She instantly finds herself in the midst of a panic attack. She knows her mother will be very angry with her if she leaves town and close proximity.

> "My mother will hate it if I move—she will
> disapprove of me if I agree with going—I
> feel guilty because her disapproval means
> I'm a bad daughter—I value being a good
> daughter—I'm dependent on her approval
> to be a good daughter."

This thought process begins with the identity Good Child. She then gives meaning to events she believes impact this definition of her. In this instance, she has said to herself that her mother's approval of her is proof she is the Good Child. Now that she is faced with disapproval, she is also faced with a crisis to her definition of self. This in turn leads her to respond negatively to the situation and begin the process of trying to solve an insolvable problem, the "rock and hard place." She now feels she must appease both husband and mother, but this isn't possible as their two interests are currently in direct opposition to one another.

In each of the examples I have moved from the initial and obvious thoughts about the event to less obvious, even hidden thoughts. This is to illustrate that the initial event isn't really the thing that generates the anxiety. There are meanings attached to this event that are the ultimate source of why an event creates such strong emotions. This is why different people respond differently to the same situation. When an event, perhaps a snowstorm while driving, occurs in the lives of two people and one responds with anxiety while the other doesn't, the anxious person is inclined to marvel at the other person's laid-back approach. We can tend to define people as "uptight" or "laid-back" when making these observations, but that is too simple a definition. It has missed the central point which is that these two people have given different meanings to the same event. That is why someone previously viewed as "laid-back" can then appear "uptight" in another scenario. It all has to do with the meanings ascribed to the event. Anxiety occurs when we give an event meaning, such as:

"There is one right answer and I need to
find it."

Or:

"Snowstorms are deadly."

But anxiety is not likely to occur for the person who gives the meaning:

"There are several good answers, so I will come up with one that seems suitable and go with it."

Or:

"I love a good snowstorm. It gives me a
chance to use my four-wheel drive!"

But deeper still, beyond the meanings we give to events, lies the reason for the meanings. This root cause is found in the identities we give ourselves. Identities are extremely important entities to understand because they are the essence of who we are. They are what give us meaning, as well as what give meaning to the events around us. We live and breathe our identities on a daily basis, powerfully, but largely unconsciously. When we understand our identity, who we define ourselves to be, we begin to understand how and why we think the way we do—how and why we behave the way we do. These understandings have enormous implications for the emotional areas of our lives, anxiety being one of them, because it is our thoughts that generate our emotions. It's tempting to stop at this notion, believing you must change how you think (what meaning you give to events) in order to change your emotions. But I know in my own life that my thoughts could not be altered just by the desire to have them change, and then to practice this change. The changes had to take place at the core of the problem, addressing identities I had taken on that were not what God had intended for me. I had to begin to understand what his identities were for me, and then prayerfully work at allowing him to change who I'd come to believe myself to be.

Identities like Rescuer, Perfectly Competent, and Good Child are excellent impersonations of virtuous and godly identities. In fact, they are not healthy identities, and I will give each a much more in-depth look in later chapters. At this point it is important to understand that identities have names. We don't just say "I have an identity", but we say "I am _____", and we give it a name. In fact, our identities are the many names by which we subconsciously call ourselves. I've mentioned just some of my own. I was Self-sufficient, Perfectly Competent, and a Rescuer. They had become deeply embedded identities within that web of thoughts and beliefs that I'd neglected to understand.

Scripture talks a great deal about names, and ties them to who that person is or who they will become as the result of their encounters with God. Jacob became Israel[6], Abram became Abraham[7], and Simon was named Peter[8] as God identified a new meaning to their lives. The first chapter of Daniel has some interesting insights on this topic. When the Babylonians besieged Jerusalem and brought back nobles of Judah, in that group were four young Hebrew men named Daniel, Hananiah, Mishael, and Azariah. All four of these names represent different attributes of God's name, Yahweh. One of the first things done on their arrival to the king's palace was to give them new names. Daniel was called Belteshazzar, Hananiah was called Shadrach, Mishael was called Meschach, and Azariah was called Abednego, all names representing different Babylonian gods. Though the Babylonian King dragged them into captivity, immersed them in Babylonian culture, and changed their names in an effort to change their identities to ones that gave allegiance to him and his gods, they did not conform. They knew who they were, and in their hearts their names never changed. All four of these young men found their identity in Yahweh. This identity, this Name that gave them their names, held them steadfast in the face of tragic and difficult circumstances.

What of the other young Israelites who the king had chosen? They were bright, brought up in the same culture as the four who singled themselves out. They were Hebrews also, yet the record shows no sign they resisted their new names, replacements for the God of their fathers. Perhaps, unlike Daniel and his three friends, they hadn't fully identified themselves with God. I propose those of us who suffer the effects of anxiety are much like these other young men. Somewhere along our own journey of faith, we've rejected our God-given names and replaced them with ones he never intended for us.

Names are our identities. Identities are who we are named. The two are inseparable. God's names in scripture are all names identifying him in relationship with us. Therefore, in naming himself, he is naming us. He is named Yahweh (ineffable or unutterable, I am that I am, above all abilities to grasp or understand, source of our life and close as our breath) and we are Human. He is named Spirit and we are Transformed, Father and we are his Children, Savior and we are Saved. When we live true to our God-given names, we reveal the defining characteristics of God as he lives out our story with us. We were created for his glory, his renown and honor. He wants to reveal all the love he has to and through us. This is an incredible inheritance that is ours to live and enjoy.

Our God-given names identify us as ones who can abide in a trusting relationship with him. But anxious people replace these names with ones that represent trust in something else, and God's word calls this idolatry. We try to live trusting in names we've given ourselves that mimic who God is and what he does, but they are harmful substitutes. These names become snares for us as we trust in our own competency as the Self-sufficient, Perfectly Competent, or Rescuer does, or as we seek our identity from the approval of significant people in our lives, as the Good Child does.

Slamming up against the wall of anxiety put the brakes on my life as I came to a complete standstill. This period, which seemed painfully useless and unproductive, was actually the first opportunity in life I took to think about who I'd become. Who we are is largely overshadowed by what we do. It wasn't until I couldn't really do anything that I became conscious of the "who am I?" question. Asking this question of other men and women who have shared a similar journey, I've learned how devastating the names we call ourselves can become and how covert their existence and influence is. These names give us identity, meaning, value, and purpose along with pain, struggle, and futility.

God's intent is that we are named as we enter into the relationship his name defines and to accept him at his word, that he will be our Redeemer, our Savior, and our Father. Who is more qualified to define us than our Creator? For me, the most intriguing part of his naming of us is the intimacy and privacy of our individual names he guards so carefully. In Revelation 2:17 we are told that one day he will give us a new name, one that only we will know. There is a mystery and secrecy around these personal names that God has yet to reveal. His intent is to whet our appetite, to help us appreciate the priceless value of this yet-to-be-revealed prize from the one who names us in our very being.

Names are precious, to be treated as such. God reveals to us in this passage in Revelation that ultimately who we are is a secret we possess with our Creator, a uniqueness he keeps in the intimacy of our bond with him. We await that name, sometimes not so patiently, but it is a name that we can't grasp for ourselves. It is a name that is a gift just as the name Child of God has been given as a gift, nothing we have earned. The name I have been given that is yet to be revealed is who God has called me to be, not who I currently appear to be. He sees me in light of this name, and only he is able to bring about the changes in me that are required to prepare me to wear it. If I knew the name I could live up to it, strive to be her, and then in my efforts lay claim to the name as mine, earned out of a life of righteousness. But we become our name as he breathes life into us, slowly, one challenge, heartbreak, trial, joy and victory at a time. We're not earning the name; he's creating us to be that name and we're not even aware of it. And so our names, his and mine, his and yours, are inseparably bound. We receive this name as we receive his grace; nothing we've earned, but what we've been given, bound up in him and the work only he can do in us.

Yet, apart from the name that Revelation 2:17 says we will one day receive, there are names we've already been given and can know because God has told us in scripture who we are, or has given us experiences that rename us. When God revealed my human frailty to me by not healing my anxiety and permitting me to crash, I gave up the name Self-sufficient and turned it in for Human. The recognition that I was frail, mortal and had no power over most variables in life saved me from wallowing in self-hatred for failure. Living within the fences of that name has taught me how to rest in the strength of God. By no means am I a perfect wearer of this name. I must return in memory often to my wilderness experience with God to remind myself of who I am when my self-sufficiency starts to rear its ugly head. He combines the truth of real experiences and the truth of his word to rename us.

We don't wear our God-given names easily because we aren't quite sure if we can trust him enough to let our old ones go. It's a decision to take God at his word, that he is fully committed to us because he said he would be, not because we earned his commitment. This brings us to a very important next step in understanding anxiety. I've discussed anxiety as a symptom, underlying thoughts and beliefs, the root cause of anxiety as being our identity, and how our identity is the names we embrace. Before I can move on to discuss the different names that often accompany anxiety, there is a barrier to receiving our God-given names that needs some serious consideration—lack of trust. If someone were to ask me what underlying thought patterns are directly opposite to trust, I would say it is those that create anxiety. Trust describes a thought and belief system that strives for complete abandon to God. When we lack trust this is in large part due to a serious misunderstanding of God's grace.

CHAPTER FOUR

Grace: Our Big Hurdle

GRACE IS NOT EASILY understood. It exists outside of our sense of reason and all rules of fairness, and this is no truer than in the life of someone who lives with anxiety. I stumbled over grace most when I read Luke 6:27-36. It wasn't just that I wrestled with what it all meant, this giving to the demanding and being kind to the ungrateful and wicked. Rather, I was almost dismissive of this passage, as if someone must have put this in by mistake. Jesus couldn't really have meant what this passage reads:

> But I tell you who hear me: Love your enemies, do good to those who hate you, bless those who curse you, pray for those who mistreat you. If someone strikes you on one cheek, turn to him the other also. If someone takes your cloak, do not stop him from taking your tunic. Give to everyone who asks you, and if anyone takes what belongs to you, do not demand it back. Do to others as you would have them do to you.
>
> If you love those who love you, what credit is that to you? Even "sinners" love those who love them. And if you do good to those who are good to you, what credit is that to you? Even "sinners" do that. And if you lend to those from whom you expect

repayment, what credit is that to you? Even "sinners" lend to "sinners", expecting to be repaid in full. But love your enemies, do good to them, and lend to them without expecting to get anything back. Then your reward will be great and you will be sons of the Most High, because he is kind to the ungrateful and wicked. Be merciful, just as your Father is merciful.

This command, Jesus explains, describes God's own behavior. In essence, this command is a self-definition of God. I found this to be quite an affront because this definition and command did not fit with the definition of justice I had held for many years. I could talk the talk about grace as well as the next Christian, but seriously, there was no way that I believed undeserving, ungrateful people should get any good thing from me or God. That was not justice and I knew God to be a just God. If God was just, that meant he would punish people for knowingly doing wrong and reward people for doing what was right. Grace was for those who earned it. That was justice. A rude clerk at the store should get fired. A reckless driver should get a ticket, but if no one was around to issue one, I sure was going to do my best to prevent him from passing me. That kid bullying my child at school, well, he needed a little of his own medicine.

Logically, it followed that I needed to earn God's favor to experience his grace and avoid his punishment, so I needed to make sure my life measured up. This is an embarrassing admission, but I really thought God was very pleased with how well I did that. I had firm convictions about what was right, and I acted on them.

The Old Testament character, Job, was very similar. As Job's suffering was prolonged and God refused him relief, Job moved deeper and deeper into his thoughts on theology as he argued his case before a silent God. Job wrestled back and forth, at one time giving praise to God, at another accusing him of cruel mockery and injustice.[9] He insisted that God had made a terrible mistake punishing him with tragedy and suffering, asserting to all who would listen that he was a righteous man, undeserving of this. It took him as long as 31 chapters to speak only what the depths of his soul knew. His righteous behavior was driven by a fear of God's destruction.[10]

Like Job, it sometimes takes long periods of pain to help us see what keeps us from real intimacy with God. It took a real crisis in my own life to realize that what often motivated my obedience to God was fear. We're afraid of what he'll do to us if we disobey. We, who are always trying to be so good, can see bad events in our lives as measures of our goodness. Either God is punishing us for something we didn't do right, or the forces of evil are attacking us because we're on track and doing so well. This is because we think God would never allow something bad unless we deserve it, and if we see no reason why we deserve it, then it must be some mistake, possibly even evil, imposing this bad thing on us. However we view our current state of deservedness, it all relies on us pleasing God and earning favor. How do you have intimacy with God when driven by fear to earn his favor? He can't possibly be viewed as safe with this kind of theology. He's to be feared, not trusted.

Maybe you can't picture yourself here and wonder how this discussion has anything to do with anxiety, so I want to give you examples of how this issue affected two women who suffered from debilitating panic attacks. They're both very different in appearance but grace was their central stumbling block.

Melissa was a woman who didn't back down from a challenge. She knew what she thought, and was very articulate when explaining her thoughts to others. She was argumentative, but good-natured, and wouldn't back away from the discussion just because it got uncomfortable. When she spoke, she gave the distinct impression she was confident of every word that came out of her mouth. She was also very convinced of her own righteousness as a Christian because she had been devout and committed to her faith, and its "rules" of righteous behavior. That was until Melissa had an encounter with prolonged and debilitating anxiety. As she struggled through this pain and had to heavily lean upon her faith for help, God began to show her that she was a very proud woman who mistakenly saw herself as personally righteous. She really hadn't noticed her pride until she saw how embarrassing she found this new "weakness"—how grating this "flaw" was to her ego even as she was weighed down by its unbearable effects. This pride disgusted her because she knew God hates its presence in our lives, and she was overcome with repentance. For the first time in her life, she grasped her own need of God's unearned grace.

Melissa hadn't intended to live this life of gracelessness. She had just found herself caught up with her own sense of ability to do whatever God was pleased with, and she unrelentingly expected others to measure up to this standard too. Convicted now of her own personal failure, she understood for the first time what it meant to fall on God's mercy and grace. She also, for the first time, was willing to let others need the same.

On the other hand, Penny, though she tended to appear self-assured, admitted that she struggled with feelings of inadequacy and unworthiness. She, too, had debilitating bouts of anxiety, and she often tended to interpret these as "what I deserve." Though she believed herself to deserve this "punishment" of anxiety, she felt in those moments totally betrayed by God, and thought that this was typical—God either not caring or deliberately inflicting this on her. She didn't expect much from him, though she was devout in her faith. In fact, she was continually striving in her spiritual walk to please God and somehow measure up, though fully convinced that she didn't. She could find herself falling into depression as well as anxiety, and she often felt very much alone, unworthy of God and his goodness, and at the same time resentful that he withheld it from her. She was at one moment convinced of her unworthiness which led her to despair, and the next confused because she wasn't sure what she'd done wrong. To Penny, God seemed mean because he refused to show her what she'd done wrong and needed to make right. He wasn't only mean; he was unfair and unjust when he related to Penny.

So if Melissa and Penny were right: if grace is something we earn through our obedience, then we can't receive it from him unless we are obedient, and we certainly can't give it to others unless they are too. Our definitions of fairness and justice have defined grace for us. We remain convinced that we can measure up, that we're capable of personal righteousness through our own efforts, and therefore others should be too. This leaves us in a quandary because we are now faced with being in direct opposition to the command in Luke 6 which is quoted earlier in the chapter. Let me illustrate in point form how I viewed this passage:

- This passage in Luke 6 does not fit with what I really believe about God's justice.
- Justice is served when punishment for disobedience happens.
- I must be obedient to earn God's favor and avoid his punishment.
- When I fail or when bad things happen, I'm afraid God is punishing me and I work hard to figure out what I'm doing wrong.
- Fear drives my obedience.
- I can't receive favor unless I earn it, so I can't extend unearned favor to others. That wouldn't be fair or just.
- I am totally confused by this passage. I must be missing its deeper meaning, or maybe it has been translated improperly.

There is another answer and, in theory, we all know it. The answer is that this command is God's actual definition of grace. It is unearned—favor without merit. Because we've been given favor without merit, we must give it to others. God goes all the way and gives us his tunic when we demanded his cloak: we've accepted praise for something he did through us and he didn't

41

demand the praise back; in anger we've struck out at him and he hasn't recoiled in anger, but accepted our blows. Luke 6:27-36 is God's description of how he interacts with us and I missed it for years. We have to stop deluding ourselves with the notion that we can somehow, in our feeble human effort, impress the Creator of the Universe so that he'll reward us. And we have to abandon this wholly unscriptural idea that he's waiting to trounce when we fail. 1 John 4:18 says:

> "There is no fear in love. But perfect love drives out fear, because fear has to do with punishment. The one who fears is not made perfect in love."

If God is love, then grace gives definition to what love looks like.

Melissa and Penny struggled with the same error. Like Job, they both saw good and bad circumstances in life as evidence of whether or not God favored them. They, like Job, both believed it was their responsibility to earn this favor through personal righteousness. Both of them stumbled with pride because they both placed responsibility on self to achieve, one believing she did, the other believing she didn't. Melissa's was obvious to her because of blatant arrogance, but Penny's was masked because of insecurity. However, both wanted to take their own achievement of God's favor into their own hands. Melissa would have argued that this was possible, and Penny would have argued that this was what she'd always been taught and couldn't shake.

Melissa and Penny both took responsibility to please God with good behavior in order to avoid bad outcomes. When their anxiety overtook them, they realized personal effort to stop bad things just didn't work. Melissa, with her tendency toward logic rather than feeling, decided she needed to test her beliefs about God for accuracy, and over time was able to take responsibility for what belonged to her: how she thought and the beliefs she held. Penny, a person who tended to rely heavily on her feelings, saw her feelings of inadequacy as proof of just that, and had a very hard time moving beyond the feeling to examine the thoughts and beliefs behind it. (The difference in approach to the examination of thoughts and beliefs is crucial to dealing with anxiety and will be discussed in much greater detail in later chapters.) Though their approaches differed, they shared in common this misunderstanding that grace is earned merit, attainable through human effort.

One night I volunteered at a local charity that houses homeless people for the night in different churches. The church recruits volunteers to set up beds, put out toiletries, and cook a meal for these folks who arrive for the night. One of the criteria for entry is that they must currently not be using drugs or alcohol. This was where I met Annie.

Annie filed into the church basement along with everyone else the bus brought that evening. I was a bit nervous with anticipation because we were to mingle at supper with these people, and I really didn't know if I had anything to say that would be of any value to them. How could I bless them when I had no clue what they'd been through? I'd never lived on the street, nor needed the skill to survive in such a hostile environment. I'd never known what it was like to fight with a chemical addiction, or protectively clutch my entire worldly wealth in a backpack. I came to serve and bless, but then I met Annie.

At the meal, as I sat at Annie's table, she told us her story. She was addicted to crack. She had started doing crack several years ago, and now toothless and frail, she recounted how she had been off it many times, only to return unwillingly again and again. She lived with a large abscess in her mouth that the antibiotics the street clinic gave her just didn't seem to relieve. Her body had no fight left in it because of the immune suppression caused by years of chemical addiction. She expressed her deepest desire to be free, and told of her wish that somehow the streets could be cleared of the dealers. She could smell the crack from two blocks away and eventually found her will to quit was undone by the slave demands of her addiction. She then had to shiver through her fevers in the cold, because she was no longer eligible for a clean, warm bed.

In the middle of her story, she surprised and delighted me with an amazing revelation. Annie told us that she knew her identity was not "Crack Addict". Yes, it held her in its power, and she would likely die under its bondage, but her identity was Child of God, and God knew her pain and struggle. His love for her carried her through her darkest moments. He loved someone who was in slavery to something that had, to this point, not been overcome. But her hope was in the future, when her body no longer held her captive. She didn't mistake her circumstances as evidence that God had abandoned her or was punishing her. Her understanding of God's grace was intact.

Annie gave me insight into the inexplicable, incalculable grace of God. God had placed me in Annie's path that night to teach me, and I was in awe of a God whose love I don't deserve, and whose laws of grace don't fit my mold of good Christian behavior. God had broken through my merit-earning mind-set with this lovely, lovable woman who I longed to see grace extended to. I came that night to serve and bless, but it was I who was blessed by Annie. I was starting to get this grace, but God still had to pull me deeper. He was about to set someone in front of me who was neither lovely nor lovable, and still insist on grace.

One summer, reading Eugene Peterson's *Tell It Slant*, God's grace was illuminated in a way that I felt very uncomfortable with. One parable Jesus tells (Luke 16) is of a manager who squanders the finances he has been entrusted with by his master. The master finds out and tells him to give an account of his business dealings, and also tells him he no longer has a job. The manager quickly sets out to make himself friends of the master's debtors, presumably to set himself up for favors he'll need when unemployed. He makes friends by further squandering of his master's funds in the reduction of the debts owed to the master by the debtors. The unbelievable part of the parable, in which Jesus is clearly pointing to God as the master, is when the master commends the manager for his shrewdness, and lets him off the hook for his wrong.

Peterson explains how this "rascal", who has used self-serving behavior to survive, is suddenly gripped by a grace that redefines him and his self-sufficient swindling. His narrow view of the world is limited by his own methods of achieving what he needs. Then God reveals a greater, more blessed view, in which the riches of grace far surpass anything he could do for himself.[11]

I don't like this shrewd manager. He's not like Annie. Yet, he gets the same grace that she does, and so I chewed and chewed on grace that summer. I knew I was uncomfortable with this view of grace, because if I wanted to receive it, it seemed I had to give it unconditionally. And I want to receive it because I'm fully aware of my need. The rub for me was that, in my mind, grace should require something that makes you deserve it. I didn't believe grace should require we have it all together, because that is patently absurd. But, at a minimum, grace needed to have some strict guidelines about deliberate behavior, particularly behavior I found very unlovable. The difficulty in my logic was that were we to apply this criterion to grace, it would no longer be grace, because grace by definition is undeserved favor. This posed me with a problem because I really didn't want to be gracious to the "rascal."

Grace isn't something you pick and choose who to bestow it upon. Yet, I still do that. I guess I'm making more of an intellectual argument than a practical one, because my life rarely measures up to what I'm about to say. From a sheer intellectual point of view, it is preposterous to expect grace, or undeserved favor, from God for your shortcomings, and then refuse to give it to others where they fall short, whether the shortcomings are in the unwilling arena like Annie or the willful arena of the shrewd manager. God gives undeserved favor to both of these people, if we are to believe Jesus' illustrations and teachings.

I remember once wrestling with God over a poor relationship I needed to address, and asking God to give me wisdom. I told him I want to love like he does, not the way I love in my own strength. As I prayed, the Israelites came to mind. I thought of their roller-coaster relationship with God over history, moving through the spectrum of obedience, to neglect of the one who called them by name and freed them from bondage, to outright mutiny. I grieved for God in that moment, imagining how hard it's been for him to love so much and be rejected so often. And then it struck me; God doesn't give people what they deserve—He gives them what they need.

God's love counts as insignificant the wrong that is done in light of the beauty he sees in his beloved. Often, it's a beauty that hasn't been realized, but God is pressed by his deep love, which we cannot ever fully comprehend, to wrestle this beauty out of us. Sometimes, the wrestle involves pain and discipline, and it feels like we're getting our just desserts. But God looks upon us not only with justice, but with mercy and grace.

In *Simply Jesus*,[12] N.T. Wright reveals the justice that is wrought by this mercy and grace. He describes justice in a way that is refreshing and enriching, rather than punitive. Wright sees God's justice as a sorting out of what is wrong with the world by healing the diseases at their source, recognizing that things aren't as they should be with all of God's creation, including those who call themselves followers of Christ. Rather than justice being an action of punishment, Wright reminds us that we are all in need of God's justice, of his sorting out of what is going wrong within us. It's not about punitive measures. Instead, "He loves in the way a doctor or a surgeon loves, wanting the best, working for life, dealing powerfully and drastically with the cancer or the blocked artery."[13]

Though we may feel that we or others only deserve punishment and our just comeuppance, God views justice as making things the way he intended them to be, and he imparts grace as he brings this about. That, he reminded me in that moment, is how to love if you want to love like him. Don't give people what they deserve; give them what they need. God's justice, the putting things right so they become what he intended them to be, is achieved through the vehicle of grace. He looks at you and me and says, "You really are a mess, but you can't fix this yourself. You need me to do it for you." This is the message of Isaiah 40 and so many other passages of scripture. I know I need this from God, and so I must be willing to give what I want to receive. Until I abandon this senseless idea that I can earn something from God, I will never recognize that those I consider undeserving can't do it either.

Grace never ignores truth. It doesn't turn a blind eye to what is really going on, but rather acknowledges exactly the state a person is in and the circumstances they are surrounded by. Grace acknowledges ingratitude is at the heart of a stingy person, that wickedness drives a man to seek out sexual gratification with a child. Grace separates needs from wants, sometimes granting wants, but always addressing needs. And this is the painful part of grace that N.T. Wright refers to, when God deals powerfully and drastically with the "diseases" of our spiritual lives. God's grace allowed me to wander unwittingly into anxiety disorder. Perhaps God's grace has exiled you from a family member because you had unhealthy demands on the relationship. Years of habitual sin, apparent or not, is something the relentless pursuit of grace will not ignore. But at the same time, God knows we are made of dust, and he's careful to give us what we need. More often than not, what we need is mercy in the midst of our foolishness, patience with our stumbling, and love that knows no bounds. This too is offered to the ungrateful and the wicked.

Isaiah 43:7 states "everyone who is called by my name, whom I created for my glory, whom I formed and made." "Whom I created for my glory" leaps off the page. We were created for his glory. His glory means he is known as he is: his honor, distinction and renown, as his character and qualities are revealed. This one thing explains why God's love is unconditional and unearned, why grace exists. If I was created to bring God glory, to make him known as he is, then I am here to allow his character and qualities to do their work on me and to be revealed through me. I'm not here to be perfection in human form, sinless and nice. I am here to show that, regardless of how hard I try or how much I fail, God's love doesn't change. I'm here to give that good news to others who are wicked and ungrateful. He is unchanging, faithful, enduring, true to his promises, and all-loving. He is using his creation (you and me) to reveal this. The mind-boggling endurance of God in the Old Testament with the Israelites is testimony to this. God isn't with us because we deserve it; he's with us because of who he is. As A.W. Tozer prayed:

> We are sure that there is in us nothing that could attract the love of One as holy and as just as Thou art. Yet Thou hast declared Thine unchanging love for us in Christ Jesus. If nothing in us can win Thy love, nothing in the universe can prevent Thee from loving us. *Thy love is uncaused and undeserved* (emphasis mine). Thou art Thyself the reason for the love wherewith we are loved. Help us to believe the intensity, the eternity of the love that has found us. Then love will cast out fear; and our troubled hearts will be at peace, trusting not in what we are but in what Thou hast declared Thyself to be. Amen.[14]

Grace, our undeserved merit, means we are the blessed recipients of God doing the work of creation for the purpose of making himself known. I've done nothing and can do nothing to deserve it. I can refuse the gift, but I can never push it so far that it will be outside of my grasp, because I'm not the one who makes it available. It doesn't exist because of what I do. God's glory and grace are deeply intertwined. Something he created (us) is to be the recipient of the benefit (grace) of his revelation of himself (glory). The church has often lost this concept, somehow twisting its beauty by taking control of this revelation into human hands. Be good. Behave. Be righteous. Be sinless. By our own hands we take responsibility for making God's glory evident. But he has told us "I am the LORD; that is my name! I will not give my glory to another or my praise to idols."[15] Still we try to snatch it from him, albeit with the best of intentions, attempting to make him known. Rather than being the vessel through which the glory is revealed, we prefer to take charge of the revelation by presenting our flawless façade to a world that doesn't know him. But deep within each of us, we know what really goes on, so we keep our secrets, present the façade, feel our shame, try harder, and fail again.

Anxious people, the masters of competency that we are, see human frailty as optional, a problem to be solved rather than the reality that it is. For this reason, we tend to bury dark, treacherous, and frightening memories of shame behind re-doubled efforts to try harder and achieve the positive results we want. But what if you and I were to stop this for just one moment and instead dive head-long into these dark places and begin to make a list of the things for which we feel shame? This is necessary because it is shame that holds us back from acknowledging all of who we are and have been, not just the positive parts. It gives us the opportunity to allow God's grace to redefine those places for us, to help us see that he doesn't view our frailty the way we do. He even loves the "us" that we find unlovable.

Shame isn't the same as the guilt that I feel to remind me I've done something wrong. Where guilt can point us in the direction of our need to make something right, or restore a relationship, shame is a deeply harmful identity of self that causes us to hide so far away that restoration cannot take place. Where guilt is about what I have done, shame is about who I am. Shame affects me like this. I did something or something happened to me, and the memory of this event stirs up extreme discomfort. It might also stir up feelings of anger or dislike, even hate for someone else, but mostly I hate that this event is a part of my life, and I would just die if I had to recount it to anyone. Even the most trusted people in my life couldn't be trusted with such awful information about me. So I hide.

One day, realizing I'd been struggling under the weight of shame for some things I'd done, I decided I needed to make a list of my shameful events. I was alone with God, and as unsafe as it felt to be totally real, I went for it. The list got long, and I was stunned to see how huge these things had become to me, though I would readily forgive or overlook them in someone else. In particular, I noticed how much of my shame revolved around things I'd said, even though many years had passed.

I stared at my own shame list for a long time. I thought about forgiveness and wondered if I could forgive myself for my own things listed there. But shame gets in the way of forgiveness. It gets in the way because it says:

- "Only a really stupid person would have said something like that."
- "Only someone who was a terrible parent would ever have had to go through that."
- "Only a bad daughter would have allowed that to happen."

The thoughts all revolve around who I name myself to be, not what my behavior was or what event happened. Some of the events are really painful, yes, but rather than recognizing them as circumstances that I was a part of or had a part in, I redefined them as my identity.

Turning something that happened into something that you are isn't a conscious decision. A child doesn't consciously process a scolding with thoughts of "I said something in public that embarrassed an adult and got me in trouble, so that thing was stupid to say, therefore I'm stupid in social settings." However, a crazy process does happen with that exact outcome, sometimes in the blink of an eye. In fact, I probably will never understand that my mind took me through this weird sequence, unless I pull out the shame, and take a hard look at it. But I am afraid to address shame, because that means I have to draw something out into the light that I would like to leave in the darkness, thank you very much.

Consequently I can live with lots of contentment most of the time, until something is said, or a reminder of that haunting event brings my shame lurching to the surface once again. It comes with such vengeance, and there is nowhere to hide. The weight of it can wake you in the night, or if you're lucky enough to sleep, it's waiting for you in the morning, following you, no matter how occupied you keep your time and mind.

Shame involves more than just messing up, or having someone else mess you up. Shame isn't just knowing you have to give an account, and that all these memories will one day come back to haunt you, however hard you try to hide them from others. Shame is a monster because we take what we've done, or what has been done to us, and say, "This is who I am. I am stupid in social settings." It is no longer something that happened or that we did. Whatever it was, it has now become my name. I do this often, not even aware it's happening. There are some things in life that I've just accepted to be true about myself. Though the pain of my name is piercing, I daily take up a ball and chain and willingly, dutifully, lock it in place on my soul. Sometimes I fight it, using logic to explain why it's not my fault that things happened the way they did, as if proving flawlessness will save me. It never does, and the name sticks. Then I have to hide yet again.

So here is the tactical brilliance of shame. Shame blocks the gift of God's forgiveness, given through grace, because forgiveness requires acknowledgment. You can't experience forgiveness unless you acknowledge that you need it. Acknowledging that you need it means acknowledging what happened. But when you acknowledge what happened, shame jumps up and points the accusatory finger and says, "That's you, it's true and you know it." Our first reaction is to hide. We look for something to make us feel better or divert our attention. It might be alcohol, food, drugs, hard work, TV, a shopping spree, or any number of distractions. Whatever it takes, we need to hide and soothe. Our identity can stay hidden as long as we can suppress, and we can suppress as long as we can find distractions. If sin is part of who you believe you are, then you cannot drag it out into the light and seek God's grace and forgiveness for it. Its attachment to you means that it will never be something God can take away—a tactically brilliant way to destroy someone.

It is these exact things that Hebrews tells us God wants to bring to light. No wonder we feel fearful.

> "For the word of God is living and active.
> Sharper than any double-edged sword, it
> penetrates even to dividing soul and spirit,
> joints and marrow; it judges the thoughts
> and attitudes of the heart. Nothing in
> all creation is hidden from God's sight.
> Everything is uncovered and laid bare
> before the eyes of him to whom we must
> give account."[16]

Aha, just as we thought! God will hold us accountable for these things and one day they'll be laid bare. Giving an account of your life is intimidating beyond words. How can anyone stand before a Holy God and give an account with confidence? A passage like this seems to give weight to the argument that God demands perfection from us and we better measure up, or the hammer will fall and we'll be found wanting.

But this interpretation ignores the scripture's whole message, and God's genuine intent. Yes, we will be found wanting. Our lives, when weighed out in God's balance, look impoverished regardless of the incredible attempts we make to be good. God turns this on its head, and again the grace of God surprises us. He tells us that he already knows we're not going to measure up, and he will help. He offers grace.

Hebrews 4:15-16 goes on to say:

> "For we do not have a high priest who is
> unable to sympathize with our weaknesses,
> but we have one who has been tempted in

every way, just as we are—yet was without sin. [16]Let us then approach the throne of grace with confidence, so that we may receive mercy and find grace to help us in our time of need."

What starts off sounding ominous and terrifying ends in deep blessing, so wonderfully summed up by Eugene Peterson:

"God does not deal with sin by ridding our life of it as if it were a germ, or mice in the attic. God does not deal with sin by amputation as if it were a gangrenous leg, leaving us crippled, holiness on a crutch. God deals with sin by forgiving us, and when he forgives us there is more of us, not less."[17]

I've acknowledged the accountability part of the Hebrews passage, and ignored the mercy, grace and help. I raise my defenses to avoid being laid bare, fearing the shame. But his intent is help, beautifully put by Isaiah 61:1-3 when he prophesied of Christ's ministry:

The Spirit of the Sovereign Lord is on me, because the Lord has anointed me to preach good news to the poor. He has sent me to bind up the brokenhearted, to proclaim freedom for the captives and release from darkness for the prisoners, to proclaim the year of the Lord's favor and the day of vengeance of our God, to comfort all who mourn, and provide for those who grieve in Zion—to bestow on them a crown of beauty instead of ashes, the oil of gladness instead of mourning, and a garment of praise instead of a spirit of despair. They will be called oaks of

righteousness, a planting of the Lord for
the display of his splendor.

Unlike me, God is not interested in giving me what I deserve. He delights in giving me what I need: to be bandaged up, freed, and released from darkness. His will is to replace all that burdens me with beauty, gladness and praise. This is God's justice. It may not be what I tell myself when I'm living in my shame, yet God speaks this good news over and over pushing forward against my fearful unwillingness to accept the help.

"For you did not receive a spirit that makes you a slave again to fear, but you received the Spirit of sonship. And by him we cry, "Abba, Father." The Spirit himself testifies with our spirit that we are God's children."[18]

Annie, addicted to crack, knew who she was. She chose to ignore the labels of her culture and the chaos in her own brain, and with childlike acceptance, received her name from God. Her body struggled under the weight of choices that she had made long ago, choices that would become her physical prison, just as much in jail as a convict behind bars. But her name was not Addict, because she knew crack was only something she was chemically dependent on. Her name was Child of God, and she could run to him for grace and mercy when failure came, and it most assuredly would. She could set her sights on him to love her through every wrong she had committed or would commit going forward, because she was his Child, who knew of her desperate need for his grace.

"You do not delight in sacrifice, or I would bring it; you do not take pleasure in burnt offerings. The sacrifices of God are a broken spirit; a broken and contrite heart, O God, you will not despise."[19]
"For this is what the high and lofty One says—he who lives forever, whose name is holy: 'I live in a high and holy place, but also with him who is contrite and lowly in

spirit, to revive the spirit of the lowly and
to revive the heart of the contrite.'"[20]

Ironically, shame prevents contrition. The sheer force of its power pushes the human heart into a destructive coping mechanism. This mechanism removes the hope that comes with acknowledgement and acceptance of failure, both in us and in others. Denial is this mechanism and it works quite effectively. Whether it's used to pretend bad things didn't happen, or used to shift responsibility to someone else for whatever bad thing that occurred, it does a swift job of letting us hide or blame. Whether we hide or blame, we've successfully removed ourselves from the work of grace that has a limitless capacity for human error. This problem brings us full circle, back to the start of this chapter. We're unable to see ourselves, in Luke 6, as the "sinners" because fear of God's wrath pushes us to denial in order to cover up those very truths.

Shame could have done two things in my life when I was first diagnosed with anxiety disorder. I could have accepted myself as a failure in life, unable to measure up to my own expectation to be Self-sufficient. I could have continued to call myself a failure, weakling, or worthless. The other thing I might have done was to slip into denial, denying that there might be some issues at the core this diagnosis, deciding it was all just genetics I couldn't control, and so I would simply rely on medications to deal with this problem, as it arose. But God's word to me from Isaiah 40 destroyed the work of shame. I could neither deny my weakness, nor wallow in the failure of it. Believing God's expectation of me was that I earn his favor, I had spent years denying I was incapable of earning it. Now, faced with the sheer reality that my life didn't measure up to perfection, God's grace revealed itself to me. I was wholly loved, imperfections and all, and wholly accepted, failure that I was. Through grace, he was showing me a new way to view him, and myself.

I was devastated the day my doctor told me I was suffering from anxiety disorder, because that meant that the woman I had always believed myself to be was gone. I had taken pride all my life in being a competent and strong-minded woman. If she had said a thyroid problem was the cause of the anxiety, it would have been much easier to accept. Instead, she told me I needed to go for counseling. My identity was crushed. God furthered this loosening of old assumptions by telling me that I was a blade of grass. His message was intended to be a direct assault on my mistaken identity.

I had to grieve the loss of who I thought I was. It was a death, and I've watched many anxious women avoid doing this. They see their improvement on anti-anxiety medications to indicate that all is returning to normal, and they launch full tilt back into the all-competent woman mode, only to crash all the harder back into anxiety. Grieving the loss of who we thought we were is an essential step in letting go of shame and denial, and embracing the grace God has to offer us. We have to come to terms with the loss, so that our life doesn't stall in the events of the past, and the names we've given ourselves.

I wonder what would happen to shame if we didn't struggle with pride and self-sufficiency. If I didn't expect myself to be more than I am, or great enough to have avoided the regrets I want to hide, or smarter than those words that left my mouth, how would shame affect me? There is an incredible freedom in confession, and I think that is why God commands that we do just that. The freedom comes not in the telling so much as in the awareness and acknowledgement that has to precede it. I am less than I want others to believe me to be. I fail, I sin, and I'm not anywhere close to perfect. Imagine for just a moment how freeing that would be. But pride holds us back. It insists that perfection and righteousness are personally attainable today, because we know how to achieve it. Thankfully, God faces us with the truth of our human frailty to turn us toward his grace: this undeserved merit, receiving from God not what we deserve, but what we need. His work is time-consuming, slow, methodical and sometimes painful. He breaks us in the places where the bone must be reset.

If we can shift our views to God's views about grace and justice, they line up beside the old thoughts with a significant difference.

Luke 6:27-36 Illustrates God's Grace	
Old Views	New Views
This passage in Luke 6 does not fit with what I really believe about God's justice.	My view of justice is wrong.
Justice is served when punishment for disobedience happens.	Justice is God putting things right for everyone, even the ungrateful and the wicked.
I must be obedient to earn God's favor and avoid his punishment.	I want to obey God so everyone's best is served, recognizing that I'm ungrateful and wicked sometimes.
When I fail or when bad things happen I'm afraid God is punishing me and I work hard to figure out what I'm doing wrong.	Grace, unmerited and unearned favor, permeates scripture. God rebuked Job for his arrogance believing he'd earned anything.
Fear drives my obedience.	Trust guides obedience, believing the God of grace looks for our best in all circumstances.
I can't receive favor unless I earn it, so I can't extend unearned favor to others. That wouldn't be fair or just.	I've received God's unearned favor (grace) and so I am free to extend it to others.

I am totally confused by this passage. I must be missing its deeper meaning or maybe it's been mistakenly translated.	I am no longer confused by Luke 6. God wants everyone's best regardless of their behavior. I can trust him with my failure.

Do you believe bad circumstances are the result of God's punishment? Do you believe you're responsible to earn God's favor? Do you secretly fear God? These are important questions, because this is the ultimate "rock and a hard place" scenario for the anxious person whose life is characterized by striving ever harder to keep up to their own personal, unreasonable expectations.

I often hear people say that they have a hard time believing God loves them individually, apart from just a general love that he has for humanity. The concept of a personal God, who treasures us, can be difficult to grasp. Ideas of worth, worthiness, and worthlessness are a regular theme bubbling to the surface of these conversations. But, we were made for his glory.[21] Our conception, birth and life were designed by God to become vessels of his glory, his character, and his manifestations of this holy, burning, and all-consuming love. We have no ownership in this creation and we can claim no hold on this love. It is God, and God alone who is the designer of this powerful display of his glory, and we, as the vessels of this grand display, also reap the incredible benefits. We are loved because God loves, is love, and cannot stop his love. We feel compassion and mercy because God is compassion and mercy, and he displays himself in us when we abandon ourselves to this display.

When we say we're merit-less, then we're on to something. When facing the God of the universe, it is a pitiable sight to see someone trying to explain their merit. We cannot point to anything in our lives as evidence we've earned what we've been given. And without merit we rejoice. How blessed are we! God has not given us the capability to earn what he gives, and words, like worthiness and unworthiness, distort the gift of God. Job felt most worthy. He was mistaken. I have friends who feel unworthy. They are mistaken. This question is not about worth, because worth has only been bestowed by the God who honors us by naming us. It is not earned.

When we focus on worth and earning our way, we aren't any closer to God than those who have no use for him at all. Convinced either of our worthiness or unworthiness, we have chosen to follow the path of gracelessness. God's great character shouts out against our never-ending pursuit of worthiness, and we're too focused on how we're doing to hear him.

Grasping grace helps us to see that our expectations are unreasonable and not from God. Grasping grace removes fear and moves us to trust the God who wants to give us new names, ones that bear only the burden we can bear, and with the strength only he can give. Grace digs deep to the core of who we are. Our identity rests in grace because God has chosen, out of grace and not what we've earned, to give us a name. What we've done is not our name. What we've earned is not our identity. Our reputation among human beings is not who we are. We are the names he has chosen for us and is preparing us to wear in the dignity that he has bestowed upon us through his grace.

Part Two

The Names That Bind or Free Us

INTRODUCTION

T HIS SECTION OF THE book will discuss, in detail, the contrast between how we name ourselves and how God names us. Each chapter will address a name commonly associated with anxiety, as well as how the name manifests itself in us in beliefs and behaviors. We'll then address the veracity of these names, their associated beliefs and anxieties, placing them in contrast to God's names and how he names us in relation to how he names himself.

God has called himself by numerous names, but we'll only specifically address some that impact our struggle with anxiety. Jesus prayed, "Hallowed be your name."[22] Hallowed means to be set apart as sacred. His names define his identities that are beyond human reach, sacred and holy. God and his names are one and the same. In whatever place or circumstance we find ourselves, we are to hallow God's names: not misuse, ignore or disrespect them. At the same time, God's names reveal to us the great value he places on his relationship with us. By naming himself, he also names us. I will discuss who he names us to be, to free us up to rename ourselves, giving up the names that lead us to anxiety.

Overcoming anxiety is a gradual process of confrontation of counterfeit names that we've allowed to define us. This confrontation is powered by truth, a daily choice to practice truth and to replace our names with the ones God has given us. It is not feasible to overcome anxiety by deciding not to be anxious, but it is a completely realistic goal to choose to fill our minds with truth. In order to do this, we need to examine names, the core of our identity.

CHAPTER FIVE

Self-Sufficient

I ONCE CALLED MY husband at work in a selfless attempt to acquaint him with the finer details of being a stay-at-home mom. I faintly remember yelling into the phone, "How would you like to work with wild monkeys all day?" Now, it may not be composed parenting to call your three-year-old son a wild monkey. He was at the appropriate developmental stage, and this required that he carry out his tireless and incessant acts of rebellion while I, his mother, trooped knowingly on. But I ask you, how many engineers do you know who would allow co-workers to scream and throw tantrums because they weren't allowed to climb up on the table and dangle from the light fixture during a meeting? I just wanted my husband to have it in perspective.

Years later, having passed the child-rearing years, I never cease to marvel at how a small child can look way up into the eyes of someone three times their size and assertively state, "NO!"

We are born with a bent toward self-sufficiency, to be masters of our own destiny and subject to none. Years of experience and training in submission to authority changes all that, of course, or does it? Though our compliance to authority or our sense of inadequacy may cause us to believe we don't seek to be named Self-sufficient, I want to explore the truth of that in this chapter. I believe that if you struggle with anxiety, it is because one name you have given yourself is Self-sufficient, regardless of how confident you are in yourself. I will explore a strong belief system associated with this name, which is the perceived need for control, the behaviors associated with it and how they impact anxiety.

The first thing my doctor told me, when I was first diagnosed with anxiety disorder was that anxious people insist on being in control. That was all she said, and I was insulted. I knew this wasn't true for me, but I was too sick to argue so I just left my thoughts unsaid. One day, I thought, I'll prove her wrong. I ended up proving her right.

CONTROL

When I've asked women suffering from anxiety if they think they're controlling, I get one of two answers. The most common answer is "No." The second one is, "Yes, because I need to be in control or I get stressed." Both of these answers reflect what these women genuinely believe, and both answers are generally untrue. The first is untrue because once these women probe, they discover they do try to control many things. They typically come to acknowledge that this is their response to life, because they know they are highly capable and highly alert to the needs around them. The second is also untrue, because stress is actually increased as we try to control things that often fall far outside of human ability.

If you answered no yourself, take a look at the following examples of indicators of need for control:

- When a loved one travels, you: are fearful they won't return home safely, monitor their flights, request they check in with you throughout the trip, and feel fearful and restless until you hear they are safe.
- You feel wholly responsible for your health, and are fearful about certain signs or symptoms, making frequent trips to the doctor only to find out you are fine.
- You have a very low tolerance for unpredictability. You don't like surprises and you're afraid that, without

careful planning. things might not go as you expect. This makes you fearful of situations you can't predict, such as travel to unfamiliar destinations, a move to a new part of the city or country, company that drops in unexpectedly, or not knowing which lane to be in well in advance of a turn you need to make while driving.

- When your child feels hurt or discouraged, you immediately see this as negative and fear this will have a bad impact on them. You attempt to get involved with whoever the offending parties are to right the wrong.

In these examples, fear of something drives a person to attempt to control the situation to keep what is feared at bay. This is why it is important for us to acknowledge our need to take control of situations. The fears that drive us to attempt to take control must be understood, because these fears are behind our anxiety attacks. Arguing that taking control alleviates fear would only be legitimate if control could be achieved. So we need to look at the situations in these examples and see if they really can be controlled.

The first two examples deal with mortality. Both are attempts to protect life, which is a perfectly reasonable thing to do. But in these examples, there is more than an effort to responsibly protect life. What is in fact being said is:

"I cannot be free of fear unless I can control death."

Example three also has a reasonable appearance, with a desire to be organized and prepared for all eventualities. However, what is actually being said is:

"I need to be able to predict what will happen in all circumstances because unpredictability is frightening."

In the final example, care and concern for a hurting child is responsible behavior, but what is actually being said here is:

"I must control my children's environment, because it is bad for them to feel hurt or discouragement."

Initially these attempts to be in control and alleviate fear seem within reason, but on closer examination, our attempt at control is really an attempt to achieve the impossible. Death is not within our control. I've lost three friends to virulent breast cancer. One of them said to me before she died that she wondered if this was her fault, because she wasn't diligent enough about healthy lifestyle habits. Another was rigidly health conscious, so believed her illness must have come because she somehow failed to appease God. How often, full of anxiety, do we run ourselves ragged trying to avoid death, fearing we're not trying hard enough?

Insisting that you can maintain predictability by avoiding things, creating structure or following certain rituals might feel good as long as this appears to work, but finally we have to deal with unpredictability. It will inevitably occur, and the effort made to prevent it requires energy that would be far better spent preparing our minds for change, so we're better able to cope with unpredictability when it comes.

Finally, we know from our own experience in life that pain is a necessary part of maturity and development, greatly enhanced when we have a wise parent coaching us on how to handle it ourselves.

There are billions of people, diseases and circumstances over which we have no control that can inflict death, unpredictability and pain. This is a reality that the Self-sufficient have a serious blind spot to. Driven by this name, we insist on placing ourselves in the seat of responsibility for things which fall outside of our control. This creates incredible anxiety, because at some level we know we're not in control, whether we're conscious of it or not. Attempting to do the impossible, we put ourselves in a high state of alertness and vigilance, predicting all possible threats and managing them, though their management is outside of our grasp.

I was someone who had no awareness of my controlling behavior and thoughts. Yet, one clue to this was that when I got sick and was entirely out of control, I viewed this as a massive failure on my part. Another clue was that I resented the sedatives because they might control me. But the one thing that really got me, that finally halted all doubts about my own demand to be in control, was the grocery store parking lot. Still sick, I sat in the passenger seat as we entered the lot, proceeded to look for the best parking spot, and annoyed by my husband's tardiness when someone else threatened to take it, I observed my reaction. I had gotten vocal and animated, my finger pointing frantically at the spot he was about to give away to that much faster car coming the other direction. My finger stopped in mid-air and I realized that my doctor was right! I couldn't even let my capable husband drive the car without help. And as I've worked with others with anxiety, I've seen the same kinds of thoughts and behaviors.

This controlling behavior is driven by the name Self-sufficient. We struggle under a belief system that tells us we should be able to accomplish things or overcome obstacles in our lives through our own effort. We believe we know the best answer and we need to take charge of the situation so things are done properly. We believe if we don't do it, it won't get done, or if it does, it won't be to the high level of standard which we know we can achieve. All of life's circumstances can be wrestled to the ground if we apply our capabilities to the problem well enough in advance. We hone our skills of prediction in order to be ready for every eventuality that might interfere with our plans. We place a high value on being inwardly strong, and when we don't measure up to this value, we have an overwhelming sense of failure. This drives us to work harder, dig deeper, and prove to ourselves and others that we can do it. If we're honest, this also leaves us on edge and overwhelmed. And when we start to know we can't achieve what we've set out to do, we're left with a sinking feeling of inadequacy.

Some people relate to the name Self-sufficient and acknowledge they've named themselves this. Others don't see it, recounting how inadequate and insecure they feel, obvious evidence to them that this isn't their name. But this is merely a matter of confidence in your achievement of the name. Both those who believe they've achieved it and those who don't value this name, some feeling they've mastered it, others beating themselves up for not having yet done so.

First, what happens when we believe we've mastered self-sufficiency? I described how busy I was prior to becoming sick. I was involved in a number of volunteer activities while raising my two young children. I often felt overwhelmed with worry, which seemed perfectly normal given the stressors I had to deal with. I would regularly wake up in the night, thinking about things that loomed even larger in the darkness. What I was experiencing was anxiety, though at the time I didn't see it as that. I would have thoughts that went like this:

> "I am responsible for a number of things—I feel exhausted and would love some rest, but this isn't possible—I can't turn any of my responsibilities over to someone else, because they belong to me—God has called me to these things and so I just need to dig a little deeper to find the energy—I am (have to be) Self-sufficient."

Having the name Self-sufficient, I was locked into maintaining the level of activity that was setting me on course for a major crash with anxiety. There was no escape route or way out because my name created a path I couldn't leave. My definition of self over-ruled the common sense that would have helped me to see I'd taken on more than I could possibly handle, and that I needed to cut back. I believed I was central to the accomplishment of good things around me, and that I could achieve things by the sheer force of will-power.

Now let's go back to Beth as an example of what can happen when you don't feel you're mastering your circumstances. Beth weaned herself off of medications and then experienced a second bout of anxiety that was worse than the first. Beth's identity as Self-sufficient remained strong, though she was continually butting up against her inability to achieve what she insisted she needed to. Two major crashes, that left her wholly dependent on family to take over all her responsibilities, slowed her down only as long as it took the medications to start working again. Once that happened, she was back to her old schedule, insistent that she had no choice but to keep trying not to be inadequate, though totally undermined by a strong sense of inadequacy.

This is how she thought:

> I'll take these medications and then things will be fine again—I have work to do, and the medication is working and making the work possible—God has given me these jobs to do—this is a divine mission and no experience with anxiety is going to shake me from it—my work can't be the cause of anxiety because God has ordained the work—if I don't do this, I'm disobeying God's expectations of me—I can't give this to someone else or I've failed God—God expects me to get these things done—I can't give this away because I am central to this achievement—this achievement is central to who I am—God expects me to be Self-sufficient and this crash tells me I'm a total failure.

Beth struggled tremendously with this. She had tied obedience to God to her name of Self-sufficient. Failure affected her profoundly because she saw it so strongly linked to God's displeasure with her. Where I pushed myself to do the impossible because of my self-confidence, Beth had a terrible sense of inadequacy because her reality wasn't matching up. What Beth and I both lacked was an understanding of God in his fullness. We felt compelled to keep trying because if we lost control, we lost the safety and security it meant to us. What we needed to do was grieve the loss of control, acknowledge the losses this would mean, and turn to God, trusting he genuinely cared for our best, though we might not agree with all his methods. We needed to educate ourselves about what his name, Yahweh, meant for us.

YAHWEH

This is the name by which the nation Israel referred to God, but it was one they wouldn't even pronounce for fear of misusing it. What a powerful example of reverence for the names of God. This name presents God to us in all of his mystery, and so I carefully wish to submit some thoughts on the name Yahweh.

Yahweh is God's name for himself, as first revealed to Moses from the burning bush in Exodus 3. In the original Hebrew, it was written YHWH. At some point, vowels were added and there is much debate about its meaning. However, most scholars seem to agree the meaning is rendered "I AM WHO I AM." The Wycliffe Bible Commentary, discussing the name's first use by God in Exodus 3:14, says that this name reveals an unfolding relationship, in which God is who he will show himself to be as he engages with us. The name defines the relationship: a mystery of revelation. "He will be to Moses and His people what He will be—something which is undefined, but which as His full nature is more completely unfolded, by the lessons of history and the teachings of the prophets, will prove to be more than words can express."[23]

When God first spoke his name to Moses out of the burning bush, he also told him to remove his sandals because he was standing on holy ground. There is so much about God we can understand from studying scripture, but there is a great deal more we do not understand about him. This is the holy ground of awe we need to stand on regularly, so that we do not lose sight of who we love, serve, and worship. Yahweh is above all, beyond comprehension, indescribable, and inexpressible: the ineffable. This is the God who is beyond all our minds can even begin to imagine. His intangibleness washes over us like the calm of the deep sea, smooth and peaceful on the surface, complex and dangerous beneath our view: beautiful mystery that soothes and strikes awe in the same breath. He cannot be contained in our finite minds. Yahweh is beyond full description.

The Hebrews understood this name to signify the God who was beyond their understanding, limitless, unlike they who were, as we are, confined to the knowledge of mere mortals. Yahweh cannot be fully understood in this place. Where he is, the ground is holy and hallowed, and our response is one of awe and great humility. Here, in this place, we absolutely must see the futility of thinking that we can control our own lives.

Yahweh is mystery. This is his undefined name of presence and power, intended to reveal just enough to provide great comfort to a people lost, broken and in need. There is a tremendous peace provided in this name at the same time as it causes perplexity and frustration. We do not enjoy the mystery. We seek to understand God in his fullness, and when we don't, we feel an intense urge to start making things up so the mystery is solved. But Yahweh is not about to be solved. He chooses not to deal with his mystery in a way which satisfies our longing for knowledge and understanding. It is difficult for us at one time to both hunger and thirst for a grasp on the mystery while resting at peace within it.

We are faced with an unimaginably complex and powerful God, whose reality reveals our self-sufficient attempts for control as the futility that they are. He tells Moses that his own humanity makes him too frail to see God's face.[24] God, passing by Moses and proclaiming his name Yahweh, makes it perfectly clear that Moses is mere flesh and blood, protected only by the hand of God.

HUMAN

Beth and I both stumbled over God because we believed we understood him, and with our understanding came the burden of responsibility to achieve his purposes in the world in our own strength. To us, this meant that if we failed, bad things would happen or good things wouldn't. It hadn't occurred to us that this was ridiculous and entirely outside of the grasp of our humanity.

God hasn't given us the name Self-sufficient. We are Human, and this is a fragile, vulnerable truth. The Lord calls us cursed if we depend on flesh for our strength[25], reminding us we are like grass that withers, or like grasshoppers, because he is the one who brings even our most powerful leaders to their end.[26] God's most eloquent speech about the vast difference between himself and humans is found in Job 38-41. That speech alone should rattle our Self-sufficient persona to its core. There is no other logical response to Yahweh than sheer humility. Humility is the natural characteristic that develops when we understand our humanity and its contrast to Yahweh. Jesus described humbling ourselves as the opposite of exalting ourselves.[27] This was illustrated more fully in Philippians 2 which expresses this amazing lack of exaltation in a God who, "being in very nature God did not consider equality with God something to be grasped."[28]

I want to illustrate this name Human by going back to when I first got ill with anxiety disorder. Prior to becoming ill, had I been asked, I would have answered I did value self-sufficiency greatly and felt pretty confident I'd attained it. In those moments, I was in the first camp, confident in my own strength. Then I became ill and I felt like an utter failure. I was devastated by my inability to function. The strength on which I had always counted was gone. I was defeated and lost. If the question about valuing self-sufficiency had been posed, I would have given the same answer with a qualification. "Yes, but I haven't achieved it." I felt such profound failure precisely because I had placed such great value on this name.

I then came to God in repentance, believing I had done something very wrong to get myself in this situation. My repentance was sincere and I asked God to show me the mistake that cost me my strength. I asked him to show me what I'd done wrong so I could right it. I was looking for the way back to strength, though I, at this point, was ready to accept a "lesser" place in God's big plan, because I doubted I'd ever return to my former self. Was self-sufficiency important to me at this point? Yes, absolutely, but I was beating myself up for not having achieved it, and this inadequacy drove me to repent, though I had no idea what for. My cry of repentance was "God, forgive me for not being a stronger person."

Then something really remarkable happened. As I was trying to understand what I'd done wrong so I could shorten the gap between where I was and where I felt God expected me to be, he came running for me. I was stuck in the place of trying to right my wrong, still attempting to achieve his favor through my self-sufficiency, when he, in grace, wrapped his arms around me and said, "Robin, you are a blade of grass." His chastisement wasn't for not achieving strength and self-sufficiency. His chastisement was for ever trying. I was undone by the limitless grace of the Almighty God. My repentance had been in the form of trying to get back on track. Suddenly I was aware that the repentance God was seeking from me was for striving to be Self-sufficient—to attain his favor and to have rejected his grace. "Repentance finally turns out to be the capacity to forego pride and accept graciousness."[29] Asking God to forgive me for not being a stronger person was repentance that was born of fear. He was looking for a repentance born of trust, allowing him to do for me what I in my own efforts would always be unable to do.

When we are overcome by the grace of God, and I mean truly overcome, we change in a dramatic way. The overwhelming response to this grace is one of love. The fear of failed accomplishment and control vanishes as we are faced with this imposing love that calls us to accept our weakness, and trust in the strength only he possesses. We aren't offered assurances that all will go as we'd like, according to our plan, but an assurance that an indescribable God loves us and will use his limitless control and strength to bring about our best. Out of love, we are able to offer our lives to him, but the offer is one of humility and recognition that merit will not be earned by a life of works. His grace to us elicits a response of devotion and trust rather than a life of works and achievement.

Pride had been responsible for my mistakes in repentance. Pride, the opposite of humility, is the exaltation of self. Of course, we've been given capabilities, a mind that can think and bodies that can act. We're not helpless and without a measure of strength. But my own bent was to see myself as sufficient to the tasks of life, no help required from outside sources. I was sure of my own capability to handle whatever came my way. In the first case before I was ill, I was too proud of my own strength to see my shortcomings that needed God's grace. Once ill, this incredible blow to my pride created feelings of such inadequacy I couldn't even grasp that God's grace could be applied to them. Pride told me that everything that I had, I had earned. Grace tells us we can earn nothing. My pride was communicating to me that I was still responsible to be Self-sufficient, and this pride manifested itself in two ways: arrogance and insecurity. Arrogance occurred when I believed that I'd measured up. Insecurity and inadequacy occurred when the reality of my circumstances told me that I'd failed. Arrogance and insecurity look like opposites but they are the two sides of the same coin—pride.

We're inundated with concepts of self-worth, self-esteem, and self-sufficiency. Pride in ourselves is deemed healthy. Yet scripture tells us pride is despised by God.

"Clothe yourselves with humility toward one another, because, "God opposes the proud but gives grace to the humble." Humble yourselves, therefore, under God's mighty hand, that he may lift you up in due time. Cast all your anxiety on him because he cares for you."[30]

This passage in particular gives me insight that there is a fundamental link between my attitude of self-sufficiency and anxiety. We weren't designed to be Self-sufficient. It does not exist within us to have that power, want it though we may. Anxiety is directly caused by us trying to meet this single-minded demand that we cannot achieve no matter how hard we try. God opposes our pride because he knows its foundation is one of self-deception. He invites us to cast all our anxiety on him. He stands ready to pluck us out of the "rock and the hard place" if we can forego our pride and accept the unfailing grace of God.

We need to view ourselves as God views us. "But God demonstrates his own love for us in this: While we were still sinners, Christ died for us."[31] We're little specks, in a universe too vast for our imagination, and yet he loves us before we even acknowledge our need for him. Were we to try on our own, we would have no way to reach him, and so he reaches out to us in all of his mystery. We do not accomplish this connection with God, but rather, it happens to us because of his grace. As long as we insist on taking charge and working for outcomes that we have decided upon, outcomes which really are entirely beyond us, we can never embrace the gift of grace. As long as we deny our own weakness, we deny his grace and we deny who he says he is.

I still struggle with pride, but I've learned how to deal with it by acknowledging it rather than denying its presence. It is constantly pushing out of the margins of my life where I try to keep it, back into the main storyline. But I can choose to continually push it back into the margins by being honest about its presence with God. When I first admitted to God that I was a proud woman, I genuinely hoped that would be the end of it. It wasn't, and the realization has helped me to be much more gracious to myself, and to others.

Human, and its beautiful characteristic of humility, is a lovely name to accept, because when we get it we're able to fit into the shoes we were meant to fill. We can embrace all the other names God gives us because we are ready to receive from his hand, without placing our conditions on him: "if you don't let bad things happen God, if you protect my family God." Humility sets us in honest standing with ourselves and with God. Masks fall away and pretenses become unnecessary. Being Human isn't about becoming nothing, useless and thrown out. The humility it brings about gives us the ability to see things as God sees them, to view our life without hiding behind walls that block our view. Humility is the state of knowing our finiteness in the eyes of an infinite God. In the moment of this stark reality, understanding our worth to him, through grace, secures our peace in the knowledge that he will not leave or forsake us, no matter what our circumstances look like. Recognition of the frailty of our humanity frees us to be exactly who we are, without the need to protect ourselves from him.

He, who is beyond description and understanding, knows us inside and out. He knows the motivation of our heart when it is often hidden from us. It is both terrible and wonderful to be so known. Someone who sees what we cannot longs to show us how to dig to find out who we really are. He doesn't tell us to fix what is wrong. Rather he says, "This is where you are right now. Will you acknowledge it and leave it to me?"

My pastor, Robert Osborne, describes confession in a way that illuminates this concept so well. He states that confession comes from the Greek word homologeo, homo meaning "the same", logeo meaning "word"—confession is saying the same word as God.

> "To confess is to get our words in alignment with what God is saying. This idea of confession, in its full sense, speaks from the truth of where we are, but it also speaks from the truth of who God is... This is the beautiful practice of getting

our words and our thoughts in alignment
with God's words and thoughts."[32]

This is what it means to be Human. It is an honest, God-driven appraisal of ourselves, as he who sees all tells us who we are. We can wear masks with our friends and family, but the long arm and deep grasp of Yahweh sees beyond all of this. There is no filter, no airbrush, and no make-up to hide behind. We are known by this one who IS, and he wants to introduce us to ourselves. Humility is the practice of letting this happen, defenses down, ready to be powerless in the grasp of his loving strength.

Anxiety at a Glance

OUR FALSE IDENTITY:

- Self-sufficient

DETRIMENTAL THOUGHTS AND BELIEFS:

- Need for control

BEHAVIORAL EXAMPLES:

- Frequent medical appointments
- Extensive safety precautions
- Excessive advocacy for those in our care
- A highly structured life
- Avoidance of new situations

YAHWEH'S IDENTITY FOR US:

- Human

Scriptures for Meditation

Genesis 2:7 and 2:22-3:7, Exodus 3:14, Job 38, Job 40:1-14, Job 41:1-11, Job 42:1-6, Psalm 8, Psalm 20, Psalm 37:23-24, Proverbs 3:5-6, Isaiah 40, John 8:58, 2 Corinthians 4:7, 2 Corinthians 12:10, Hebrews 4:14-16.

CHAPTER SIX

Perfectly Competent

I T'S NOT OFTEN YOU meet the near perfect embodiment of a name, but Cathy was as good an example of Perfectly Competent as you'd ever find. Having recently moved to Canada, she found herself overwhelmed by all the changes moving had brought for her. Anxiety was a constant companion and she put it all on the shoulders of the adjustments of her move, but over time came to see that this was only the tipping point for a life that was ripe for a crash.

An educated woman, Cathy knew all the answers. She could enter into conversation on several topics, and even liked to take on topics about which she knew only nominal facts, stating them with such authority that it was hard to question her knowledge. If anyone did challenge her, she was ready for the debate. She was entirely un-teachable because she felt she must always appear to know the answer. Even when corrected, she'd just nod as if she already knew what she was being told. She admitted to me that being wrong was nearly impossible for her to accept.

Cathy became heavily involved in volunteering shortly after moving. She ran a community program, volunteered at school, and was quickly awarded a leadership position on a committee to choose a new pastor at her church. It was important to her that her community understood the competency and skill she had to offer, and so she made herself known in all her new circles.

Cathy also had to have the perfect home. Her carpets were vacuumed in rows, her sheets were ironed, and her windows sparkling. She never had a spare moment to rest, but she said she enjoyed being busy rather than having idle time on her hands. She did say she wished she could sleep better, as she often woke in the night, her sleep regularly disturbed with a busy mind working through the details of the next busy day. But this, she reasoned, was just a normal part of being a highly responsible person. Her house was perfect, her appearance was perfect, her community contribution was perfect, but she had one real stressor that seemed to be eluding this perfect execution.

Cathy spent a great deal of time in school, meeting with her kid's teachers. She stayed on top of all their homework, knew every weakness they had, and worked hard with them to overcome these. She regularly questioned the teaching abilities of the teachers, and feared that her kids would one day be total failures in life, all because of the poor understanding the teachers had of her children's learning needs. She was continually concerned that they would be sent ahead to the next grade without an excellent understanding of every subject, even though they were still only in elementary school. She waffled between seeing them as gifted and, therefore, unchallenged by the teachers, and seeing them as struggling with some subjects because they weren't bright enough. Ultimately, she admitted, she felt they should be able to achieve high marks in every subject or the school was failing them.

Though Cathy had an extreme case of Perfectly Competent, and not all anxiety sufferers would relate to her, the one thing she had in common with everyone I've talked to about anxiety was the need to find the ONE RIGHT ANSWER. It's so important to a Perfectly Competent person, it deserves a headline.

I have always hated to make mistakes. When I've been restless with troubled thoughts, they were often about mistakes I'd made. I could even be troubled over mistakes someone else made because of the impact it had on me, telling myself I should have known better than to trust them, or to have found myself in a situation with them. In many areas of my life, either trivial or significant, I was extremely tough on myself if I thought I'd gotten the wrong answer. All logic aside, without even realizing what I'd done, I had, for many years, attempted to live up to the name Perfectly Competent.

Perfectly Competent is a close relative of Self-sufficient and has its own struggle with the two-sided coin of pride. This name provides ample opportunity for anxiety to creep in, and though similar to Self-sufficient, it branches out from self-centeredness to draw in those around us. People outside of us are the focus as we become consumed with how we are viewed by others. With this name, we'll explore three belief systems: control, approval, and blame, the behaviors associated with them and how they impact anxiety.

CONTROL

We've discussed control in the preceding chapter in depth, but there are some examples of controlling behavior that are specifically related to Perfectly Competent. Here are some examples:

- You wish you could delegate things to other people because you're swamped with things to do, but the truth is, you can't afford the risk. They won't get it right, so delegation would mean that you'd have to supervise everything they do and correct mistakes, ending up in more work for you.
- If you do delegate, you hover.
- When faced with a problem to solve, you have a tendency to believe in one "right answer" that you are responsible to find.
- Your sleep and spare time are regularly interrupted by thoughts about how you can achieve perfect execution of solutions to problems.
- You tend to see things as black or white, right or wrong, with little room for gray areas.

Within each of these examples, there is an element of fear that is driving the insistence on the right answer. In the first two points, the fear is that we believe we know exactly what needs to be done, and are therefore solely responsible for making sure it happens. These thoughts appear to ooze the self-assurance of having attained Perfect Competence. Here's an example of how the thoughts progress:

> "I want to be viewed as Perfectly Competent—I have the right answer—I also have the right way to achieve the right answer—no one else knows what I know—no one else can do it as well—that makes me wholly responsible—I have to do it myself, or supervise closely whoever is doing it."

In the third and fourth points, the fear is that the right answer might be missed, and so more and more effort must go into finding it. This is where we struggle with self-confidence. We feel the need to act in a perfectly competent way, but worry we won't be able to achieve it. Here's what we're thinking:

> "I am supposed to be Perfectly Competent—that means I better find the right answer and make no mistakes in the solving of this problem—what if I don't pick the right answer—I need to make sure I've thought of everything—if I act and haven't made the right choice, I've failed to live up to who I am supposed to be."

Finally, in the fifth point, the fear is that we, or the world around us, will get out of order if we don't have a strict set of guidelines and formulas with the right answers. This final one lends itself to rigid and legalistic approaches to life which take on, not only the responsibility of self, but the responsibility of keeping everyone else in line. Here are some examples of how this thought pattern affects faith:

"I'm Perfectly Competent when it comes to doctrine—I've got all the right answers about what Christian conduct looks like—I guard myself very carefully to ensure I live up to this conduct at all times—I, being the bearer of such knowledge, am responsible for everyone around me—I must always be ready to hold people to account."

These are all examples of how insisting on being Perfectly Competent leads to controlling behavior. This controlling behavior is driven by the belief that perfection and "one right answer" are our responsibility to bear. This sense of responsibility drives the fear of failure, which creates anxiety. Our fear is reasonable, given what we're insisting we need to accomplish: a life of perfect execution in whatever arena we insist on that perfection.

When we name ourselves Perfectly Competent, we become obsessed with the "right answer." Believing it's out there, we work hard to find it. Sometimes we're absolutely confident in our answers and sometimes we're not. When we're not, we have to work that much harder. It's a "rock and a hard place" scenario, and we need to look at how we arrived at the conclusion that this achievement is our responsibility and within our capability.

This conclusion is rooted in our sense of need to earn favor and merit from God, and again reminds us we've not accepted the gift of grace. While a Perfectly Competent person MAY be able to extend grace (though this is often not the case) to someone else, they most certainly cannot extend it to themselves. They demand that they must achieve right living by effort and work, following rules to the letter, ensuring right outcomes, and guaranteeing they've left no stone unturned to find what that is.

Without conscious awareness, the Perfectly Competent person has placed on their own shoulders, and often the shoulders of others, accountability for earning the favor of God. They'll cite proof texts such as "Faith without deeds is dead"[33], and "Be perfect, therefore, as your heavenly Father is perfect."[34] Yet this Perfectly Competent person goes on to miss the central message in just about every parable Jesus told—we cannot attain our own righteousness. It isn't about choices we make; it's about the choice God made long before we were born. Nothing we do earns this favor that he has decided out of his own love and mercy to extend to those willing to acknowledge their need of him. This is offered before we even acknowledge our need.

I will go back to my own encounter with God while sick. This was my own prodigal story, in which I had the opportunity to see myself in both sons of this parable[35]. In the previous chapter, I recognized myself in the son who had gone astray at the outset of the story. I was coming back to God in repentance for my lack of strength, certain God would help me be stronger again if I could just get it right this time. I had no idea what that meant as I had no idea how I'd lost my strength or how to get it back. But I had this intense sense that I'd totally blown it or I wouldn't have found myself in such a dire crisis, unable to cope with the simplest tasks of life.

In the Prodigal Son parable, the father came running for the son, stopping him from asking for a hired-hand position, refusing the solution to the problem the son was about to suggest by offering him so much more. Unwilling that I should stay mired in the misguided repentance of the inability to stay strong, God came running for me and offered to be my strength, refusing my request to show me how to get it back myself. In this lesson God also wanted to dismantle the other name, Perfectly Competent, as he was about to reveal to me how I'd lived much of my life like the obedient son.

I had worked hard to get God's approval, faithfully serving him with all my right choices and loyal good works. I was earning his favor with my righteous acts, and I wanted credit for it. No, I deserved credit for it. This was the Perfectly Competent, self-made Christian woman who God was obliged to recognize and reward for faithfulness. How blatantly foolish that looks in print, but deep within me, I felt my righteous living had set me in good standing with God. He challenged me, first to give up my insistence on strength, and then to recognize that I could never make all the right moves and earn his favor. His grace was the final offer. No strength or personal righteousness I possessed had ever impressed him to offer a gift he freely gave out of his own decision, not mine.

Now the stakes had changed. If I couldn't impress the God of eternity with my righteousness, maybe I wasn't the necessary solution to every problem. Maybe it was okay not to know all the right answers. Maybe it was okay to let others make mistakes too. Maybe, when others disagreed with me and my rules, they might've been right and I might've been wrong. Just maybe it was safe to let go of control.

This release from responsibility for perfection in righteous execution, pulls us out of the "rock and hard place" we have insisted on placing ourselves in. We have, in futility, assumed we could earn God's favor and control our world through righteousness, right answers, right living, etc. We've ignored the prodigal son message, the many mistakes of King David, and the rag-tag, broken hoards that flocked to Jesus, who told them it was human and perfectly acceptable not to have all your stuff together.

This insistence for the "right" answer is downright debilitating. First, we experience the mental anguish involved in trying to figure out the impossible. Then, there's the anxiety of having reached a decision, acting on it and wondering if we acted too soon, not waiting long enough for the right answer to arrive. Then, when faced with any kind of opposition or criticism, we lay awake at night ruminating over this wrong thing, or just as pointless, come up with elaborate come backs or plans to convince dissenters that they are wrong. Over-thinking and over-working the problem just deepens those useless, futile ruts that become our mind's home.

APPROVAL

There is another thought pattern which plays a significant role in this identity. The Perfectly Competent person wants not just to be recognized for competence, but to gain approval from others for it. Seeking approval has become so much a part of decisions and behaviors, that the awareness of this may not even be obvious. It isn't until the competent person is threatened with loss of approval that this becomes most clear. For this reason, Perfectly Competent has an even greater hold on us than Self-sufficient, because we add the power of others to decide if we live up to our name.

It's important to remember that a Perfectly Competent person doesn't expect competence in everything, but rather in things that they have given priority to. Understanding whose approval we seek, and for what, helps us understand where we've placed our value for competence. Here are a few examples:

- Overnight visitors mean endless amounts of work. Meals have to be prepared from scratch, or the house must be free of obvious signs of dirt. You want your guests to see you as a highly competent host so you must put in a great deal of effort to prove this to them. It's exhausting.
- You know you spend long hours at work, but when it's time to go home, your boss, as well as some peers, are still working. You know you need balance in your life and your family is important, but you find yourself staying longer and longer for fear you'll be considered less devoted to your work than others.
- You believe you need to convince people of a decision you made, and find yourself giving endless detail about the rationale for the decision you came to. Even though this decision in no way affects them, you want them to approve of what you decided. In fact, if you were to be honest, you often monopolize

a conversation with endless detail, seeking to prove your competence and win approval.

- You're with a group of friends and they are debating a topic important to you. You stay silent and refuse to give your opinion for fear you'll say something inaccurate or that will be shot down. You'd much prefer to be safe than to have anyone in the room think you wrong or foolish. Though you feel strongly that you're right, you're also afraid you might be wrong and the thought of someone believing you're wrong horrifies you for fear you'll be ridiculed or disrespected.
- You're often in the thick of an argument, frustrated when people refuse to accept that you're right.

These examples help us to see ourselves in situations where we are actually trying to gain approval for perfect competence, or hiding our fear of incompetence from those we seek approval from. Everyone has a different set of skills they value and place priority upon. For example, the host values cleanliness and home cooked meals above relationship with guests. The other examples reveal a need for approval for their accurate opinions and decision making, though they go about handling it differently. It isn't so much that we need to understand what we seek approval for and from whom, though this is helpful, but we need to understand that we are willing to allow the opinion of others to impact us more than whether or not our behavior is healthy.

We all know people who get very anxious at the thought of having company. They don't sleep well, anticipating all the things that have to get done. They worry about what foods to prepare, spend hours in fatigue and frustration making food or cleaning house, and by the time company arrives, they're exhausted and extremely stressed. The desire to be seen as a Perfectly Competent host, and given accolades for it, leads the host to extremes of both performance and exhaustion. We will engage in ridiculously excessive behavior in order to get the approval of others, even if it does lead to an anxiety attack. We have given ourselves an identity we must at all costs protect, and one of the measures we use to gauge our success is whether or not we're approved of by others. Who we believe ourselves to be is within the power of someone else to judge. Knowing our inability to control what they think, we have yet again placed ourselves in an impossible predicament.

When we seek approval, we discover that saying yes to one thing means we must say no to something far more important to us. The competent host has no time for relationship building with guests when they finally arrive. Things have to get done. The boss's approval means your family must be said no to, though you know your time with them is of lasting value. If the conversation is centered on your competency, you drive away intimate relationships because most people soon tire of you. Finally, when you won't let others see you as you really are for fear of what they'll think, you prevent depth of relationship and intimacy. All of these costs are in the form of relationship, a loss of priceless value driven by our insistence on naming ourselves Perfectly Competent. Rather than risk the imperfections of sincere human relationships, we seek to control them by controlling other's view of us. The implications for anxiety in this effort are clear, not to mention the great loss to us in relationships of depth and vulnerability.

BLAME

Not surprisingly, the tendency to find blame is another thought pattern that fits in with the name Perfectly Competent. The bar is set so high that failure is inevitable, and so blame can always be ascribed to either self or others for this failure. Those who name themselves Perfectly Competent can tend to be very impatient and critical of self or others when there is failure to measure up to whatever standard has been set. When others fail to measure up to our standard, we're quick to criticize them and rule their behavior as inexcusable, "righteously" indignant that their behavior is inferior to our own. When we've failed our standards, in our frustration we can look to find others to blame for our failure. When others can't be found, we beat ourselves mercilessly for failure. We're willing to give lip service to forgiveness, but certainly not without an adequate amount of remorse and proof of understanding of the grave ramifications of making a mistake.

This harsh stance has to do with what is at stake for the Perfectly Competent. Failure means loss of identity. Yet, though failure is a real threat, there is a sense of superiority with the Perfectly Competent that demands these standards for both self and others. It's a conundrum, and a panic attack waiting to happen. Blame is the inability to reconcile high standards of perfection with the reality of life. Blame is a denial of the truth that mistakes will be made, accidents will happen, and people will even intentionally mess up. This must be integrated into our world view so we can have an adequate response, rather than one that insists on the impossible, deteriorates into rumination of what should have been and who is at fault for it not being that way, ultimately leading to anxiety.

Now that we've looked at how our thought patterns associated with the name Perfectly Competent work, we need to understand how God has addressed this in scripture. If you're like me, you'd prefer to get a self-help book that can show you how to get the imperfect under control. And this is never more evident than when we struggle with anxiety. When I meet people who are in the midst of a crisis with their anxiety, often the first thing they seek is some kind of formula for how they can get out. We like the structured plan, just as in other areas of our lives, confident in our competence to find our way out. Were God looking for perfection, though, he would have given up on the human race early in Genesis. As scripture walks us through God's history with mankind, it reveals the futility of our efforts for perfection with the truth of who we are. That truth doesn't reveal Perfectly Competent people, but ones that regularly fail to live up to the ideals they wish they could achieve.

Our real struggles begin when we use the flesh to battle the flesh, which is the response to human frailty that Perfectly Competent people rely on. We sin, make mistakes, fall and then turn around and apply the same flesh by working harder, or forcing self-restraint and legalistic rigidity to the problem. Instead, what we need to do is trade in our might and willpower to show the world what righteousness, competency, and perfection look like, for an open-handed, undeserving posture of willingness to be shaped by the Lord. What a gift if we could allow others the same freedom. This work within us is the work of the Spirit of God, not our own, and we cannot enjoy the benefits of his life in us as long as we insist on achieving our own form of "right"eousness.

SPIRIT OF GOD

The Spirit of God is an enigma to me. He is a mystery, like the wind, and where he comes from or goes to is unknown. The Spirit represents my overall experience of God in this tangible and sensate world. There is nothing solid for me to grasp or comprehend about this being. He is ethereal and celestial, beyond what my physical senses, which I so heavily rely upon, can perceive. Spirit is a difficult concept to understand in a physical world where we live with the tangible. And yet, there is a deeper comprehension of him I cannot define for someone else. This comprehension, though it happens outside of my physical experience, is intensely real to something deep within each of us if we're sensitive to it. This is one of the profound mysteries of God; the Spirit of God rests upon us, or more mysteriously yet, lives within us.

Here is a concept which I cannot wrap my brain around, yet somehow I experience within. God lives in us. He is outside of us and around us, that I get. But God lives in us. At the core of our being, the Spirit of God resides. "Do you not know that your body is a temple of the Holy Spirit, who is in you, whom you have received from God?"[36] My own spirit, that I sense but cannot understand, does not live alone, but resides with the Spirit of God within me. This is what God's word tells us, but it is a vast and unfathomable concept to intellectually reconcile, and so we often neglect to respond to this wonder in order to let it transform us the way God tells us only he can.

In scripture when the Spirit rests on or indwells someone, most often there is a supernatural change that takes place in that person. When Saul was anointed by Samuel as king, he was told the Spirit would change him into a different person.[37] In many references to the Spirit in scripture, the Spirit caused people to start prophesying as happened in 1 Samuel 19. The Spirit is described as unfathomable and beyond instruction.[38] He instructs us with truth and wisdom.[39] He is full of wisdom, understanding and knowledge[40], he is present everywhere[41], and he promises never to leave us.[42] He gives life[43], and freedom[44], intercedes for us beyond our ability to understand, and he has the power and strength to lift us out of our weakness.[45] One of the most comprehensive discussions of the Spirit of God and the manifestations of his Spirit is found in 1 Corinthians 12-14. Here Paul makes it clear that the manifestations that come through us cannot be credited to our efforts, but belong to God.

The Spirit is jealous and relentless in his pursuit of our hearts. He knows no limits, understands our every thought even when we don't, and can lead us on our path to eternity. "Where can I go from your Spirit? Where can I flee from your presence...Search me, O God, and know my heart; test me and know my anxious thoughts. See if there is any offensive way in me, and lead me in the way everlasting."[46] This Spirit is unending in his invitations, and though we continue to push him away or try to ignore him, these invitations persist, and the circumstances designed to promote willingness continue: from blessings, realized dreams, to discipline, brokenness and pain. He speaks in a gentle whisper at times[47], and at other times in the powerful confrontations that were Job's experience. This is no vaporous push over.

There is no room for duty and personal righteousness when confronted with the Spirit of God. They are only fakes of the real thing, and God who knows the heart, knows what is real and what isn't. The Spirit knows how to develop real, substantial and breathing fruit. Life by human effort can't manufacture this fruit. Somehow, when we should be enjoying the lavish gifts of grace and gradual change wrought by his divine work in us, we turn the story on its head and think we'll go out into the world and do big things for God. We've forgotten that this humanity is about a God who is big, doing big things for weaklings. We hate our weakness and so we strive to be great. We even ascribe good motives to this by reasoning that our intent is greatness for God. However, it is in our recognition of our weakness, and there alone, that we become fully his. We then grasp the meaning of Karl Rahner's prayer:

> You must adapt Your word to my smallness, so that it can enter into the tiny dwelling of my finiteness—the only dwelling in which I can live—without destroying it. Then I shall be able to understand; such a word I can take in without that agonizing bewilderment of mind and that cold fear clutching my heart. If You should speak such an "abbreviated" word, which I could grasp, then I could breathe freely again. O Infinite God, You have actually willed to speak with a word to me! You have restrained the ocean of Your Infinity from flooding in over the poor little wall which protects my tiny life's-acre from Your vastness. Not the waters of Your great sea, but only the dew of Your Gentleness is to spread itself over my poor little plot of earth.[48]

I have a passage of scripture which I love to return to again and again to remind myself of what I am able to control.

"Trust in the Lord with all your heart,
and lean not on your own understanding.
In all your ways, acknowledge him and he
will make your paths straight."[49]

The reason this passage is so meaningful to me is because it sums up something major that occurs throughout God's word, which is full of promises to us. In this passage God is revealing how to understand our role in all things. This is my paraphrase:

"Here is what you have to do—this is
your job in life. Trust me with everything:
your life, your sin, your daily needs, your
relationships, and your flaws. Acknowledge
me in every part of that, good and bad.
Here is what you must <u>not</u> do. Lean on
your finite understanding to figure out
how to live this life. And **here is my job.**
I will make your paths straight."

Say that last sentence with all the different emphases and let his promise sink in. *I* will make your paths straight. I *will* make your paths straight. I will *make* your paths straight. I will make your paths *straight*.

These words are process words, not instantaneous achievement and overnight success words. This is God's slow and gradual work-in-progress that denotes our entire earthly life.

TRANSFORMED

In all of these references to the Spirit of God, something happens within the recipients of the Spirit. They are changed, not of themselves, but by the inner work done in the divine power of the Spirit of God. Yet with all the evidence of this work throughout scripture, we rarely live as if we expect he can bring about changes in us that are outside of our ability to influence. Certainly scripture is clear that, for the most part, our willing participation in allowing God access to our lives is necessary. But the work that happens within us belongs to the Spirit and is not ours to lay claim to.

2 Corinthians 3:17-18 is the passage that I've chosen to help me rename myself because of who the Spirit of God is:

> "Now the Lord is the Spirit, and where the Spirit of the Lord is, there is freedom. And we, who with unveiled faces all reflect the Lord's glory, are being transformed into his likeness with ever increasing glory, which comes from the Lord, who is the Spirit."

I'm in the process of being transformed into his likeness, not there yet, and certainly not through my own competence.

Another verse I often remember when I start succumbing to fear or temptation says "He (I prefer she) who dwells in the shelter of the Most High will rest in the shadow of the Almighty."[50] I will repeat this verse over and over, trying to allow its truth to penetrate whatever currently seeks to draw me away from God and my peace in him. One night, as I was meditating on this verse, it suddenly occurred to me that the shelter of the Most High is actually me. I am his dwelling place, and so wherever I am, so too is he. Struggling with whatever it was that brought me to this verse that night, I pondered what it would look like if I stopped wrestling my anxious thoughts, these adversaries of my peace, and just rested in the divine power of God as the verse instructs.

Madame Jeanne Guyon, a Catholic mystic who lived in France in the 17th century, addresses this idea of living life by the Spirit rather than flesh.

> Temptations, as well as distractions, are a major problem you will encounter at the outset of your adventure into God. Be very careful in your attitude toward them. If you attempt to struggle directly with these temptations, you will only strengthen them; and in the process of

this struggle, your soul will be drawn away from its intimate relationship with the Lord.

You see, a close, intimate relationship to Christ should always be your soul's only purpose. Therefore, when you are tempted toward sin or toward outward distractions—no matter the time, no matter the place, nor the provocation—*simply turn away* from that sin. And as you turn, draw nearer to your Lord. It is that simple. What does a little child do when he sees something that frightens him or confuses him? He doesn't stand there and try to fight the thing. He will, in fact, hardly look at the thing that frightens him. Rather, the child will quickly run into the arms of his mother. There, in those arms, he is safe. In exactly the same way, you should turn from the dangers of temptation and *run* to your God... You and I are very weak. At our best we are *very* weak. If you, in your weakness, attempt to attack your enemies, you will often find yourself wounded. Just as frequently, you will even find yourself defeated.[51]

These words are true for our temptations to sin as well as our temptations to get life right in our own strength. Perfectionists find the idea of the slow, gradual work of God's Spirit to be unsatisfactory at best, and unlikely at worst. So, they set about reforming and conforming to standards which they wish to attain. One example in my own life of how I tried to achieve perfect competence was in the area of anxiety itself. I genuinely believed that the anxiety that threatened to overtake my mind could somehow be controlled by my will. I blamed myself, believed I just needed to work harder at finding a solution to the problem and to be competent at the execution of it. But this is exactly why we struggle, solely because we cannot conform ourselves to make the struggle go away. Ironically, the insistence on perfection increases the power of the very things we wish to overcome. As we focus on the offending problem, it begins to have greater control over us.

The Spirit is capable of manifesting in us that which we are unable to achieve for ourselves. Yet, we try so hard to overcome in ourselves the very things we repeatedly prove unable to overcome. We attack our fears or our temptations with strategies and coping mechanisms that give temporary relief at best. This repeated effort occurs because Perfectly Competent is believed to be integral to who we are or who we need to aspire to be. We're compelled to keep up this fight because to fail is such a severe blow to self. But God's Spirit seeks to redefine our Perfectly Competent selves into the Transformed, which occurs on his terms.

Two things had to happen in my life before I was willing to exchange perfect competence for the work of transformation that only God's Spirit could do in me. First, I had to admit that I wasn't Perfectly Competent. A crushing bout of anxiety made this first step relatively simple. But the second step was much tougher. I had to then acknowledge that perfect competence wasn't even possible, and that it had been an elusive and unsustainable identity. This proved to be much more difficult because the identity had so long been a part of what I believed was necessary for me to have value.

Jesus set the bar impossibly high (be perfect[52], easier for a camel to go through the eye of a needle than a rich man to enter the kingdom of God[53], turn the other cheek, give your tunic as well as your cloak, do good to those who mistreat you[54], love your enemies[55]) so that not only his disciples, but also the self-achieving perfectionists who led the religious elite could see that this identity is impossible for humans to obtain. We are called to a standard that we are entirely incapable of achieving. Grace is our only hope, and genuine transformation can come only after

that grace is accepted, and is entirely possible only because
work of the Spirit of God.

I knew I ran a terrible risk if I gave up achieving this for myself
and chose instead to be Transformed. I knew he might not change
me in the areas of my life that I most wanted it. I knew I would
have to give up conveying myself as someone with the answers
and start being a listener ready to learn. I would have to become
very vulnerable because I would no longer be in control of my own
reputation. I had to fall on God's mercy, and trust him with the
outcomes. I knew he might not choose to transform me the way
I wanted. Could I live with the possibility that some of my daily
internal woes would not be miraculously removed from me? Did
I trust that he knew what he was doing? I had to learn to abandon
my notion of flawlessness for one of willingness. I needed to say,
"If you are willing, God, I am willing for you to do what it takes
in your strength to make me whole." My job was, and is, a daily
commitment to willingness.

Willingness is within our power, but flawlessness is not.
Perfection will not be achieved over your lifetime, or in daily
decisions, or in moments when sin creeps in and seduces you.
But change, the kind that is unexplainable and permanent,
gradually takes shape in the life of someone who learns to wait in
expectation for what the Spirit can do. Things that once seemed
to hold us captive lose their power when we look to God to do
his transforming work. It's frightening, turning control over to
someone so ethereal and mystical. The only requirement of us is
trust, though this is no small feat. But what is our alternative?
Abandoning the work of achieving perfect competence means
giving up on something we never had control of in the first place.
Replacing it with trust in God's Spirit means we still don't have
control, but now we've given up one lack of control for another
that is genuinely trustworthy.

Choosing the name Transformed, rather than Perfectly
Competent, gave me a new set of thoughts. Where once I had
insisted on finding the one right answer, agonizing endlessly over

finding it, I could now peacefully choose an answer that seemed reasonable, and trust God to right my path if he felt it necessary. I began to resist the urge to think there was only one answer, that all other answers were less than adequate, and that I needed to figure it out for everyone else. Instead, I started to humbly recognize mystery, ambiguity, and diversity as valuable parts of life. I began to accept myself as a student of other's life experiences, rather than their teacher. I began to challenge my black and white, rigid and legalistic thinking with a recognition that gray areas exist, and it's okay if I don't know the answer. It turns out that I'm not the world's moral monitor anyway. I can trust that the Spirit of God is as much at work in others as he is in me. And I'm still working hard at swapping the approval of others for genuine relationship, where I let people see my flawed self and I don't hate myself for it. Instead of always blaming others or myself when my standards of perfection aren't met, I regularly remind myself life is never going to be without mistakes and errors and one right answer may not be worth all the great lessons in making a few mistakes.

It would be a scary thing to let go of all the former if we were changing our name to Chaos, or Anything Goes, but we aren't. We're trading it for the name Transformed, and so we let go to someone who is able and willing to take the reins out of our hands. We have within us the Spirit who is capable of a transforming work, to overcome on our behalf the things we are powerless to do, as well as to choose what needs work and what doesn't. This is how we remove ourselves from the responsibility of solving what we are not able to solve. This is how we release ourselves from the grasp of the anxious tension between what we demand of ourselves and what we can, in reality, achieve.

Psalm 37:24 tells us we will stumble even though we belong to God. It isn't a command to stumble, but it is simply a statement "though he stumbles..." God knows we will stumble. We get so worked into a lather when we do, but God isn't surprised by any of it and offers the solution. We "will not fall, for the Lord upholds (us) with his hand." The Lord upholds us with *his* hand. All the time we're busy trying to be better people, get things right, and stop messing ourselves up, the Spirit of God knows only he can make these things possible. It's an amazing freedom to realize we will stumble and God isn't upset by this. He's just going to make sure we don't fall beyond hope, and he'll do it with his own hand, not ours. My job is to *run* to God. I can't feel loving when I hate, I can't stop lust, I can't stop fear and anxiety, and God is fully aware and entirely at home with this idea because he knows he can, in his time and his way. The greatest temptations before us are nothing in comparison to the one *not* to run to the Spirit of God.

I can remember the hopelessness I felt when I became ill from anxiety. I wondered if I'd ever be my old self again, and I doubted I could ever recover and overcome anxiety. My doctor confirmed this fear by telling me I'd live with this problem off and on for the rest of my life. That's what happens to us when we have to rely on human strength. We resign ourselves to whatever help we can give ourselves as sufficient enough. My doctor, in kindness, tried to help me accept a life where anti-depressants and coping skills would be my help.

Though filled with doubt at the possibility of overcoming this sheer, unreasoned panic which threatened to snuff out any lucid thoughts I had, I couldn't get over the idea that hope existed for me. And it did. My road out of anxiety disorder wasn't quick and painless. What was most painful was to come to terms with my helplessness in this struggle, regardless of the help and relief the doctor could provide. These only controlled the problem. I knew I couldn't personally get control over this issue, and I threw myself on the mercy of God to help me. I honestly didn't expect anything to happen, but as he convinced me more and more of my inability, he also wiggled the need to control myself out of my own hands. He expects us to acknowledge our weakness and then let him do what we can't.

I no longer live with the panic that represented much of my life. Though it's not realistic to expect the things you wrestle with to miraculously leave you forever, those things can become only niggling annoyances that remind you of your weakness and your need for God. This happens through the work of God's Spirit as we give him carte blanche, with us doing only the extremely difficult but necessary work of relinquishing control to him. This is no small thing. I remember thinking "But what if he doesn't do it", though I wasn't exactly showing success on my own. But my only other recourse was to accept someone else's claim that this was always who I would be. When we do that, we have resisted the work the Spirit can do in our lives, the power and delight he has to transform those he loves.

Romans 8:9 tells us we are controlled by the Spirit if he lives in us. This is not will-power, but a supernatural Spirit at work inside a vulnerable, yet transformable, human mind. It is a work outside of human comprehension because it transcends our abilities and knowledge. This is not a work to be grasped or replicated by some other means. It is the miraculous work of a Spirit who has the capacity to be in all places, giving life and freedom to all who allow this work to take place. It's absolutely baffling to our human imaginations, and precisely why we need to acknowledge our need. We just can't replicate this!

The key role we play, in this work of the Spirit being done, is obedience—setting of the mind on active decision and choice to pursue obedience to the Spirit, recognizing all the while what Paul did; we still remain in imperfect human vessels. But Galatians 5:22-23 tells us what fruit we will begin to see when we set our minds on this. The "fruit of the Spirit is love, joy, peace, patience, kindness, goodness, faithfulness, gentleness and self-control."

Years ago I memorized this passage believing I was responsible to "do" these things, berating myself when I failed. I decided for myself what kindness looked like, what joy should be, and how to love others. Then I would set about doing these things so I could be a good person. It wasn't until God revealed my weakness to me, in my time of deep distress, that I began to understand that this is not a "to-do" list, but a list of outcomes that naturally occur when

I stop trying in my flesh and just purpose my heart on obedience. I'd like the fruit to happen but it doesn't because I make a decision that it will. That's because it's not my fruit. It isn't something I can grasp and call my own. It's a gift that the Spirit gives to me as I struggle in my humanity toward obedience. He brings about the fruit from my one choice—obedience. Obedience requires listening. Life by the Spirit means we constantly attune ourselves in the quiet, meditating on him and his word, waiting before acting, seeking wisdom, and silencing the distractions around us that drive us to believe we must act now. No small feat for a capable person who has always tackled life and gotten things done.

Paul warns us, with great severity in all of Galatians, about what happens to us when we veer off this life by the Spirit, allowing personal accomplishment and works to distract us. There is within us a disquieting force that presses us on to action. It's not pleasant or peaceful, but it is a humanly rewarded and revered quality. We call it perfectionism. What greater compliment can be paid to someone than to say "you're a perfectionist?" Who doesn't love hearing that? Though it may even be said to us as an admonishment or warning, our human ears pick it up as a compliment. We love to hear ourselves so named, and it becomes for us something we strive ever harder to prove ourselves to be. But this is not God's name for us. Instead he calls us to be transformed by a work of grace, something outside of our ability to control or will, other than to yield ourselves to its strength.

Anxiety at a Glance

OUR FALSE IDENTITY:

- Perfectly Competent

DETRIMENTAL THOUGHTS AND BELIEFS:

- Need for control
- Need for approval
- Ascribing blame

BEHAVIORAL EXAMPLES:

- Obsession with finding "right" answers
- Insisting we know the right answers
- Tending to be rigid and legalistic
- Seeking relationships based on approval of behavior, rather than transparency and depth
- Blaming someone (self or others) when things don't go according to plan

THE SPIRIT OF GOD'S IDENTITY FOR US:

- Transformed

Scriptures for Meditation

Zechariah 4:6, Romans 8:1-17, Romans 8:26, Romans 12:2, 2 Corinthians 3:4-6, 2 Corinthians 3:17-18, Galatians 3:2-5, Galatians 5:4-5, Galatians 5:22-26.

CHAPTER SEVEN

Good Child

STAN LEE, WHEN INTRODUCING the world to Spiderman in the 60's, wrote "With great power there must also come—great responsibility."[56] These words are the great burden for that Self-sufficient child of chapter five who looks up into the eyes of an adult and asserts "No!" Assuming they are all-powerful, some children can go on to a lifetime of assuming responsibility for a parent or family member they so assertively believed they controlled in childhood.

Jean Piaget (1928) coined the term "magical thinking" in his work on child psychology. Children in the years between two and six believe they are central to their world, have no understanding of cause and effect apart from themselves, and therefore believe they are the reason things happen. This is why many children at this stage of life believe they are to blame if their parents divorce. This magical thinking can lead children to attempt superhero efforts to bring about happiness in hurting adults in their world.

Surely, this is only a stage that passes and doesn't stick with adults who have moved into the age of logic and reason. Yet, when we are talking about this new name, the Good Child, I would argue that we haven't actually moved out of this magical thinking stage. We often stay stuck in this place after having made ourselves responsible at a young age for a parent we came to believe needed us. We believed we were the only person who could help them, the only person capable of making them happy, and we have kept this belief, even when logic and real outcomes proved otherwise. In fact, the reason we've been unable to weigh this name against logic and reality is often because we haven't understood we've so named ourselves.

I just recently did a bit of magical thinking. I was at a funeral where a dear friend was giving the eulogy. She had asked for prayer because she didn't want to be overcome by emotion and embarrass herself. As she began to speak, so, too came the tears. At first I prayed, but then I reverted to a cheer leading stance "Come on Judy, you can do it. Come on, I know you can." She couldn't hear my inner words, but somehow I just kept saying them as if they had some power. Or how about when you're sitting beside your husband in the stands at a sporting event and his body shifts jerkily in his seat as if to magically make the players on the field move in the direction he moves. We have this illogical tendency to believe ourselves influential over a world we are genuinely powerless to control.

While these examples are harmless and common, there is a place where this type of thinking is deeply ingrained and causes us to take responsibility for meeting the needs of members of our family of origin, often a parent, by being everything we think they need us to be. Believing at a young age, when magical thinking is rampant, that a parent needs us embeds a belief that we are somehow responsible for them long before they become unable to care for their own needs. Before we move into the thinking of the Good Child, we need to address this issue of needs because it has a central place in how a Good Child thinks.

Needs are an important part of our life, but we're often not even aware of what they are. When I meet people who are anxious, I often ask "Do you know what your needs are and how to meet them?" I usually get a blank stare back. Many anxiety sufferers have virtually no idea what their needs are. If you have no idea what your needs are, it's a pretty sure bet you don't know how to make sure they're met.

When I refer to needs, I am not talking about the essentials for existence, like food, shelter and clothing. I'm talking about the emotional, social, intellectual, spiritual and practical needs we all have, beyond our basic need to survive. Emotionally, some of the needs we have are to know we're cared about, supported, loved and understood. Socially, we need to belong and receive emotional needs through family, our community, religious institution, friendships, and romantic relationships. Some examples of intellectual needs are to broaden our thinking, to be challenged to creativity and change, and to be productive. Some of our spiritual needs are met in private time with God, in spiritual conversations with friends and family, time spent in church, and time spent engaged in meaningful activities that add value to our communities. We also have practical needs that must be addressed, such as exercise, proper rest, time and resources to meet mundane daily needs like bill paying and grocery shopping, or access to assistance when we're not skilled to repair a dead furnace in the middle of winter.

Needs often aren't something we think about intentionally, but we still instinctively know we need to meet them. However, when we don't take the time to understand them, or if healthy ways of meeting needs have never been modeled to us, we can go about meeting them in ways that are unhealthy. This is the problem that surfaces for the Good Child, as well as the parent or family member she is taking responsibility for. If neither understands their own needs, how to meet them in appropriate ways, and who is ultimately responsible for doing this, a Good Child will end up assuming all responsibility without giving it a second thought. This happens with cooperation, perhaps even expectation, if the parent shares the belief that the child is, in fact, responsible to meet their needs.

This list of needs is, of course, not complete, but helps us understand what categories of needs we have and the numerous ways we meet them. There is no such thing as one source for meeting all needs. There is also no such thing as someone else being responsible to make sure that a capable individual's needs are met. Yet, these are two mistakes the Good Child makes. First, he takes responsibility for meeting a certain set of his parent's needs (mistaking a parent's unwillingness to meet their own needs for inability), and second, the Good Child assumes he must be the ultimate, if not only, source through which this can occur. We again meet the "rock and the hard" place scenario. We end up creating impossible situations from which we absolutely must extract ourselves if we want the freedom to enjoy our relationships without becoming anxious within them.

If you struggle with anxiety, the name Good Child may resonate with you as it does with many anxious people. Their value in life came early from the identity as a Good Child. Certainly, other relationships were highly significant to them, but they made a discovery that their loyalty to this name had the power to override other loyalties that might have a greater claim on them, even interfering with their marriages. Using this image of magical thinking helps us understand how a grown adult comes to develop these loyalties to a parent to meet the parent's need. Having for so long believed they were capable of relieving whatever strain they saw on their parent, they have come to assume full responsibility.

Here are a few questions to help you identify whether or not this is a name you have given yourself:

- Do you feel responsible for your parent/parents when they are unhappy/un-approving/in a mess?
- Do you regularly feel guilt on account of your parent/parents?
- Do you struggle with decision making when poised between loyalty to your parent's wishes and those of your spouse or another significant relationship?
- Do you recognize that your parents are responsible for meeting their own needs unless they are physically and/or mentally incapable (not unwilling)?
- Are you able to discern the difference between their inability to meet their own needs and their unwillingness to do so?

- Do you experience a resistance from your parents when you try to "fix" them, yet you still sense they want to keep you involved in their problem?

Giselle realized she had named herself Good Child and that it had contributed to anxiety. When she tried to deal with the problem, she met with incredible resistance from her parents and siblings. She was raised in a family with parents who fought regularly and openly throughout her childhood. Her dad was viewed by Giselle as authoritarian and distant, unwilling to meet her mom's emotional needs. Mom was viewed as the victim of her dad's distance, and the siblings had various roles in dealing with this problem, Giselle's being that she was responsible for meeting her mom's emotional needs.

I've seen this identity of Good Child in a number of people who suffer with anxiety. While your story may be different than Giselle's, as you read it, look for some similarities. In her own words, this is how Giselle defined herself as the Good Child while still a child in the family, living at home:

"I had to be there when my mom needed me. This meant I should listen, encourage, support and defend her (against my dad)."

After she moved away and was raising her own family, she continued in this role. Believing her job was to carry this heavy load for her mom's sake, she thought of herself as her mom's confidante and counselor. This meant that no matter what her relational responsibilities were elsewhere, when it came to her mom she:

- Needed to be available.
- Had to be on her mom's side if her parents argued.
- Had to let her mom "dump" on her whenever she needed to.
- Had to be there for her mom (meaning always ready to hear her problems) if she wanted her mom to be there for her.

- Was never to make her mom feel responsible for her own life and choices.
- Must anticipate her mom's emotional needs (learn to read between the lines).

For Giselle the name of Good Child was an identity of such great responsibility that she believed she must be present to her mother's emotional needs at all times, making herself available to her mom even if that meant stretching herself thin for other relationships. Her identity as a Good Child was further compounded by her mom's reactions when Giselle failed in her responsibilities. She was able to read her parents expectations that she be the Good Child when:

- If she said she saw her dad's point, her mom would fire back with the question "whose side are you on?"
- Her dad, after having fought with her mom, would call Giselle and tell her she needed to call her mother because she was in need of comfort. This job was clearly hers, not his.
- After working up the courage to tell her mom she wanted to be her daughter, not her "go-to" person to fix her mom's pain, her mom took this as rejection.
- Though she would tell her mom she didn't want to hear about what her dad had done wrong, her mom insisted she listen, and expressed hurt and disappointment with Giselle's lack of caring.

The pressure Giselle placed upon herself to carry her mom's burdens was great enough, but when she realized her feelings of responsibility weren't healthy and attempted to address the problem, the pressure was compounded by her mom's reaction. Both the guilt she felt when she couldn't "fix" her mom's problems and the guilt she felt at her mother's accusations combined to bring about serious anxiety for Giselle.

> I was trying to carry something, feeling responsible for something that wasn't my problem. It required my emotional

and mental attention to the point where I wasn't able to function in a healthy way for my own family (husband and children). Setting healthy boundaries (with my mom) made me feel like a very bad daughter. Subsequently I would suffer an anxiety attack. I was always trying to figure out the right thing to do, because if I did the "right thing" then obviously everyone would be happy. I had two people at war within me—the Good Daughter who wanted to do the "right thing" and the broken woman who knew that things had to change in order to be healthy—mentally, emotionally, spiritually and physically.

God designed us for relationship. He himself is wholly relational and spends our lifetime pursuing a relationship with us, calling us by name. Genesis 2:18 is our first glimpse into God's design. "It is not good for the man to be alone." Relationships are God ordained and God created, the opposite of "not good." God, above and beyond us, embodies the concept of relational. And he designed us to be like him. It is absolutely essential to be in strong relationships. Where we run into trouble is when those relationships define who we are based on another's approval, or the approval we give ourselves for having achieved desirable outcomes for another person.

APPROVAL

Giselle required her mom and dad's approval to believe she was a Good Child. Mom's approval was given when she made herself available whenever her mom wanted to talk and when availability meant unquestioning support of whatever position her mom took. Dad's approval was given when she provided this support to her mom, relieving him of any need to support his own wife. Though her dad's approval wasn't as important to Giselle as her mom's, it became an extension of her mom's approval. This was the gauge Giselle used to know if she was being a Good Child. By choosing this name for herself, Giselle gave them the power to judge her success at the core of who she was—her identity.

Here was her thought process:

> "Mom is miserable—Dad has wounded her again—I can comfort her—I am responsible to fix the effects of Dad's callous behavior—I will soothe the wounds and comfort Mom with love that Dad won't give—Mom will approve of me—I am a Good Daughter."

Giselle thought she had the ability to relieve her mom's sadness and meet all of her unmet emotional needs. This perceived ability led her to feel responsible. As a Good Child, having the ability and the responsibility, she was then accountable to her parents for this great feat. This was magical thinking. We cannot, regardless of how hard we try, no matter the tools or tactics we employ, meet all of the emotional needs of another person. The logic Giselle needed, to honestly look at her own power and responsibility to make her mother feel loved and supported, was entirely clouded by this magical thinking. She had never taken this thinking out of the recesses of her mind and analyzed it for accuracy. In reality, Giselle never could make her mother feel better.

Giselle's mom's problems never changed and the situation never improved. Her mom continued to feel rejected and uncared for by her husband and continued to demand sympathy and nurture from her kids to make up for what she felt lacking. Rather than see that her own efforts weren't working, Giselle worked harder and harder. Having handed her mom such great power to judge her, Giselle had no option but to work harder at achievement of what would make her mom approve of her. Seeking approval for something she was powerless to accomplish, she found herself increasingly anxious, demanding of herself that she solve the unsolvable.

This problem belonged to Giselle's parents. Giselle was a grown woman who had moved away from home, and her parents were both capable of managing their own personal lives and the needs they had. But Giselle was so tied to her identity as Good Child, this never occurred to her. When things didn't work out for her mom, Giselle felt overwhelming guilt because she was failing as the Good Child. Her guilt made it impossible for her to even consider that her expectations of herself needed to be re-evaluated.

CONTROL

The Good Child is not the only identity at play here. Giselle's Self-sufficient identity affirmed "something has to be done and I am the person to do it." Being Perfectly Competent drove her to seek out the right answer after every failed attempt to right the wrong. I asked a question earlier; do you experience a resistance from your parents when you try to "fix" them, but still sense they want to keep you involved in their problem? The resistance comes when the Good Child jumps into these two other identities and begins to try and control her parents. This is met with resentment from the parents, which equals disapproval, but the identities of Self-sufficient and Perfectly Competent drive a person to take charge of her parent's needs. For Giselle this might have taken the form of researching counselors in her parent's area and calling one to set up an appointment, calling her mom's friend and asking her to spend some time with her mom, or calling the pastor and asking him to intervene. But her mom wasn't seeking help from anyone but Giselle. And her mom would have also felt legitimate indignation at Giselle doing things that hadn't been asked, or for which permission hadn't been granted.

To this point we've talked about three thought patterns that are hidden in our names and that we're unable to analyze for accuracy. They are control, blame, and approval. These thought patterns run through our identities, and continue to build upon each other. Giselle's guilt came not only from her failure to meet her mom's approval, but also from the inability to change her mom's situation and to come up with the perfect answer to make that happen. These unreasonable responsibilities became the source of incredible anxiety for Giselle. But there is also another thought pattern that was adding to the problem. It was dependency.

DEPENDENCY

Dependency occurs when both the Good Child and the parent believe, without question, that it is the responsibility of the Good Child to meet needs of the parent. This may also lead to a mutual dependency, each believing they should be able to rely on each other to meet these needs. If we have no idea what our needs are and how to meet them in a healthy way, it is easy to slip into dependency on someone who we feel safe with. Just because you've never identified your needs doesn't mean you don't feel them and instinctively search out ways for them to be met. It takes conscious awareness of what needs are and who should be looked to for meeting them to avoid unhealthy dependencies.

Giselle alluded to this when she insisted that she had to be there for her mom if she wanted her mom to be there for her. Giselle also struggled with dependencies on her mom to do the same for her. But to be clear, this was not simply a caring relationship where they could share burdens with each other and walk away knowing they'd loved and supported one other. This was a bond that kept them tethered to one another even after the conversation ended. Both felt an enormous responsibility for the other's emotional needs, as well as an expectation from the other to meet their emotional needs. Believing this was their only safe place, they became isolated from other relationships that would have helped meet needs that could never be met within this bond.

Fear drives this isolation and can lead to the outright rejection of any other close relationships.

This type of dependency is an unhealthy bond with another person that seeks to overcome fears you don't want to address and deal with in a healthy and beneficial way. Instead, you prefer to soothe these fears with the proximity, either emotionally or physically, of another person. I am not referring to normal healthy relationships that rely on one another for support, love, and positive interdependence. I am referring here to the use of another person to attempt to meet needs that cannot otherwise be met because of fear. Dependency is used to quell these fears, rather than to address the crippling effects they have on us.

Here are five fears of dependency:

1. Fear of rejection.
2. Fear of aloneness.
3. Fear of the unknown.
4. Fear of confronting problems head-on.
5. Fear of being revealed/discovered.

Though this list isn't exhaustive, it provides a jumping off point to understand our own fears as they relate to dependency.

The power of fear of rejection cannot be overstated. It is crippling. It prevents us from engaging in the social situations we must have for health. Within the relationships we do allow, fear of rejection can cause clinginess or cause us to lash out in rejection before someone has a chance to reject us. This fear can be related to real experiences where rejection has occurred and has been extremely painful, particularly because it happened in the formative years of youth. Sadly, this fear then goes on to become a behemoth in adult years that prevents a person from believing they can be in trusting, open and honest relationships with a number of different friends and acquaintances. This fear of being rejected causes a person to build around them a protective and isolating shell, limiting social contacts and friendships, keeping acquaintances shallow and superficial. Those who fear rejection often have a tiny circle of relationships, and those relationships are characterized by clinginess and insecurity. This insecurity is what leads to the preemptive strikes of rejection I referred to. In order to avoid the pain of rejection, this fear will drive a person to powerfully, sometimes with great hostility, reject someone who they fear is about to reject them.

Giselle's mom saw Giselle's request to bring health to their relationship as an outright rejection of her mom. This led her to lash out in hostility, rejecting Giselle, labeling her a Bad Child, believing Giselle's imminent rejection of her to be a real threat. In actual fact, Giselle had no intention of rejecting her mom as she sought out a healthier relationship. What happened, though, was that the relationship ended almost entirely, and only because her mom refused to accept Giselle as a daughter under any new conditions. Viewing the request as a precursor to rejection, her mom responded with the first rejecting strike.

The second fear, of being alone, is a logical next step when we believe we will be rejected by people. It then becomes imperative that we cling to the relationship or small circle of relationships we do have. Often these relationships are confined to family, because within a family it is possible to use manipulation to keep the members from leaving, either emotionally or physically. A family member who lives close by can make dependence possible because they are physically present to be with a person. A family member who lives a great distance away cannot be physically present, but that doesn't prevent an emotional dependence from occurring. There are still methods of keeping in touch and dependent relationships can be characterized by manipulation, often through the use of guilt. "You never call" or "you never visit" are used to keep physically absent family members emotionally present. For the family members who are physically close, there are many opportunities for guilt to be employed because contact is so frequent. Helplessness to look after tasks around the home, or expressions of loneliness and sadness impact the Good Child's guilty conscience. Also, a parent can remind the child of their duty to the parent. This is often the rule in families where fear leads to dependencies and family members aren't expected to be responsible for dealing with their own fear or finding healthy ways to meet their own needs.

The third fear, of the unknown, expresses itself in unwillingness to try anything new. Unless a situation can be proven safe and predictable by the dependent person, the situation will be avoided entirely. Perhaps they can be persuaded to try something if the person they depend upon will take them along, but sometimes this won't even work. Dependent people can be so fearful of new situations that they won't go on holidays, leave their home, or enter a situation that they feel is unfamiliar. The less you try, the more things that remain unfamiliar, and the cycle continues.

The fourth fear, of confronting problems head-on, leads to passive/aggressive behavior. A dependent person will accept being uncomfortable or unhappy with behaviors from those they are dependent upon, without speaking up. What if Giselle, knowing her mom was lonely, decided she would take her mom to a community event and introduce her to friends, then encourage her mom to follow up with these friends? This might seem like a viable solution to Giselle, but her mom would find this terrifying. She wanted Giselle to help her with her loneliness, not strangers. Not only would she resent Giselle for not just meeting her need for companionship herself, she would feel that Giselle was treating her like a child. But for fear of saying something that would push Giselle away, her mom would remain silent in her anger.

Though passive about addressing what Giselle was doing, her mom might refuse to go to church with Giselle next week, or not call Giselle for a few days when the regular routine is at least one daily call. She'd send a signal that she wasn't happy with Giselle in the hopes that Giselle would read her mind and recognize that she'd made a "mistake." Giselle's mom would refuse to deal in an open and effective way out of fear that she'd lose contact with Giselle, employing instead the use of strong hints.

The fifth fear, of being revealed or discovered, leads to great isolation for the dependent person. In an effort to hide the things they are sure others will reject them for, they isolate themselves to avoid this pain. This can be done by avoiding social contacts or by engaging in them, but creating a protective barrier that doesn't allow for vulnerability, openness and transparency. The shame discussed in Chapter Four is often behind this fear.

Dependency is a self-perpetuating problem. The very fears that dependency tries to protect are the same fears that dependency creates the reality for: another "rock and the hard place" scenario. When we fear rejection, our behavior is so defensive, hostile or fearful that we drive people away from us because our fear-based behaviors are so objectionable. When we fear we'll be left alone, our clinginess becomes a repellant to people wanting to get close, because closeness poses risks of suffocation. When we fear the unknown, we isolate ourselves from exposure to new people and new situations that will broaden us and keep us socially and emotionally fed. Without this exposure and experience, new situations become more and more terrifying because we get no practice trying new things and finding out we're okay. When we are afraid to confront problems head-on for fear of losing someone, we hide our feelings, fester with anger, and never deal with people in honest ways that promote strong relational bonds. Wild emotional outbursts are a natural outcome of keeping a lid on frustrations, further driving people away. Finally, when we fear being discovered or revealed because we expect to be rejected for our flaws, we refuse to let people into our lives and so we're still alone. Dependency becomes a vicious, self-perpetuating cycle of destructive behavior, fraught with fear and anxiety.

A Good Child is set up for anxiety in any dependent relationship. If dependency were a gas tank, it would always be empty. There is no limit to the amount of support and concern that must go into that tank, and no amount of support and concern can fill it. The destructive cycle of dependency, its poor behaviors reinforcing its fears, makes filling of the tank impossible. No amount of effort on Giselle's part could create lasting healing. She found herself working harder and harder to achieve something that was impossible, but because of her name, Good Child, she couldn't give up. She then spiraled into panic attacks because she insisted on solving the unsolvable.

Often, a Good Child can feel entirely responsible for a parent, while quite capable of seeking out their own healthy and supportive relationships elsewhere. However, it can be the case that the Good Child either engages with the parent in a mutual dependence, or has a distorted view of how to develop healthy relationships. This may lead to clingy and possessive relationships, but can also lead to distance from people because the Good Child doesn't know how to have relationships without feeling responsible to control people's happiness. This is just too exhausting.

When the Good Child has engaged in mutual dependency with the parent, this becomes a template for other relationships. The fears of dependency we discussed (rejection, aloneness, the unknown, confrontation, and being revealed) also plague the Good Child. These fears make social settings places of great potential danger, reinforcing the need for the "safety" of the dependent relationship.

In summary, the Good Child is susceptible to anxiety in at least three possible ways: by insisting they achieve approval from a parent for being the Good Child, by attempting to meet the never ending dependency demands of a dependent parent, or by not engaging in healthy relationships because of their own predisposition to dependency. These are all "rock and the hard place" scenarios, where expectations are impossible to meet. God didn't create these expectations, though a Good Child would be the first to argue that point. Scripture has a lot to say about God as the ultimate parent. He is named our Father, and we are Children of God. These identities contrast significantly with the name Good Child.

FATHER

Christ had a great deal to say about our Father. Prior to Christ, the name Father was rarely used for God in scripture and when it was, it was far less personal. Christ, however, referred to him as a personal Father on several occasions, outraging the Jewish religious leaders of his day. They saw this familiarity with God as blasphemy because of their high regard for God as separate from humanity. Applying this name to the Almighty wasn't reverent or religiously pious enough. Calling God his Father put Christ on too equal a footing with God, and this incensed the religious convictions of his contemporaries. Christ was making reference to the Ineffable as someone that could be recognized in a familiar, familial way. The implications were enormous, and changed the landscape of the spiritual condition of man. A father has children who enjoy a very special and intimate place in the family, and Christ told us many things about our Father's loving and intimate attitude toward his children.

The claim was astonishing and disturbing for a culture that wouldn't speak God's name aloud for fear of misusing it, and the descriptions of the nature and character of the Father a challenge to all they believed, yet deeply comforting for the many that were weighed down by the rules and demands of their religion. Jesus opens the door wide when he talks of the Father, treating God as a family member, with qualities children wish for from their dads. But this was not the first time God had been described with such intimacy among the Jews.

King David, in his poetic, boyish exuberance, gives us one of the most elaborate depictions of a Father who knows, with intimacy, the needs of his creation. David delighted in a childlike trust and love for God, daring even to express all of his deepest anguish when he felt alone, angry, or ignored by God. Psalm 139 is a moving portrayal of a loving God. It describes the intimacy and fondness of our Father, that he knows our inmost being, knit us together with detail, care, and great insight about our needs for development. He lays his hand upon us and knows our thoughts before we do. And all of this wrapped in mercy, fondness, provision, love and forgiveness. A human father, doing all he can to be a good man, can only poorly reflect what God, as our Father, wishes to give to us. This is complete comprehension of our human souls, no secrets hidden, sandwiched between love that wants to meet our needs and grace when we need it most.

Jesus names God "Father", rounding out this picture that David has, years before, painted for us. He tells us our Father is perfect[57], loves his enemies[58], knows our needs before we ask[59], has a special fondness for children[60], and cares about the needs of his creation.[61] He assures us that the Father will not let us be snatched from him[62], that he is unwilling that any should perish and will seek the lost[63], and that he is pleased to give us his kingdom.[64] This is an intimate picture of an intimate parent.

I grew up without a dad. I had some uncles, but I didn't really spend much time with them because they lived a distance away. The men closest to me were in the day home I went to everyday, the sons of my babysitter, who became like older brothers to me. They were very dear, though mysterious, and sometimes quite intimidating just because they were male and unexplainable. I distinctly remember hiding around corners, terrified yet oh-so-curious, about the male visitors that would come to my babysitter's house. These new males, usually boyfriends of her daughters, sent me scurrying in fear to the nearest safe place from which I could observe their strangeness. Peaking around hall corners, I watched them carefully. Sometimes they tried to talk to me. I was gone in an instant.

I never grew up with a father that destroyed the dream of a good father for me. Some people can't say that, and for them it is difficult to feel safe with God the Father. But I always sensed that he parented me, along with my mother who did an excellent job of loving and caring for me, teaching me the value of life: my own and others.

Still, somewhat surprising to me because of the caring mother that I have and love, I always dreamt of a human father. I don't know if every little girl dreams of being the cherished one in the eyes of her dad, but I did. I met my dad when I was just barely an adult, and the man was doomed from the outset because he could never live up to the dream that many years had created. Over the years, though I grew to love my Dad, I finally let go of the dream. It was a crushing thing to realize my dad would never have a deep understanding of who I was and how I was like him. He had not had the experience of getting to know me as you do in a child/father relationship, and the ties could never be strong. I had expected too much from a man who couldn't have lived up to my imagination.

The kind of father I wanted was someone who knew me: my loves, my dreams, my flaws and imperfections, and who loved me for every one of them, all the more because there were glimmers of him in even those. I wanted to be protected and sheltered, at the same time as I wanted to be pushed to be more, and challenged to overcome my fears. I wanted a great strength I could look to for guidance on the hard paths of life, for comfort when things were going sour, and for courage when I felt it least. I wanted someone to smile at me with a love so deep, that no matter what I did, I was always okay with him. I was looking for a superdad.

The day that the light finally dawned on this unattainable dream, I was devastated to learn that this father didn't, and couldn't, exist. Something precious slipped off the shelf of my life and was shattered into a million pieces. This precious thing, so dear and so meaningful, was now in shards that could never be restored to their former place of honor. For days, I struggled under the weight of a loss of something that was no more than a fantasy. And then, in the midst of my broken-hearted state, it occurred to me. I had missed it for so long. That someone that I had dreamt of was God. He was my Father. He had always been there, fulfilling every one of those dreams, yet unnoticed by me.

No words capture the profound impact when I realized that the infallible, indescribable Creator of the universe had taken on that role, when I was looking for a mere mortal to do it. I let go of an imaginary hand so that my hands were free to clasp the hand of my Father, who holds me fast.[65] It is the richest blessing to find that the deepest desires we have for a good father are mere shadows of our Father. Could these dreams be his invitation to seek him? He calls each one of us his Child, and he waits for us to take our part in that relationship.

CHILD OF GOD

Jesus challenged us to develop childlike dependence on God. It's a bit awkward to think of ourselves as becoming like a child. After all, we spend years teaching our kids to "grow up." We take great pride in independence and maturity in our adult world. We take responsibility for ourselves and are much frowned upon if we don't. So what in the world did Jesus mean, and how do we become Children of God?

When raising my kids, I liked to imagine that my job was to wean them off of dependence on me, and onto dependence on God. When they were little, their dad and mom were the final authority, but my hope was that we could successfully convey that this authority would end, and then they needed to choose to let God take over the role of directing their lives. I was shooting for independent adult kids, but at the same time I wanted them to grow into dependence on a flawless Father who can always be trusted, unlike the limited human parents they'd known. It's a dependency that can be nurtured and fostered because it involves thinking for yourself and taking responsibility for what you can do, while submitting to the leadership and authority of a God who can do all that you can't. Scripture tells us he knows us better than anyone could, and that he, because of his great love for us, continually looks out for our best.

Children don't have all the experience and capability to move through life alone. There are many things they can't do, and though they don't often recognize this, they need parents to do a great deal for them. But the same is really true for us as adults, too. It's not about sitting passively, waiting for permission to live, but rather, living with the recognition that we don't have all the answers and that we need help from someone who does. When we weigh what we know against his knowledge, we have so much to gain from dependence on our Father.

I want to look at how the thought patterns of approval and dependencies are met head-on by this name. First, let's take a look at approval. If God approved of what you were doing, choosing, thinking, or saying, but no one else did, would he be enough? I struggled with anxiety in no small part because my own answer was "no." It wasn't that I didn't care about loyalty to God. It was, rather, that I had a set of prescribed rules about what loyalty was, and I based these rules largely on what other people approved of in me. I wanted to be a Good Wife, Good Mother, Good _____. Fill in your own blank. These names were, to me, synonymous with Child of God, because I viewed my ability to measure up to these as proof that I was loyal to God. I got the cart before the horse on this one, not unlike the rich young ruler in Luke 18:18-30.

At first glance the story of the rich young ruler is an example of Christ's view of wealth. But there is actually far more going on in this story, and author Kenneth Bailey does an amazing job of illuminating this. He writes with the perspective of years of personal experience in Middle Eastern culture in order to bring the fuller meaning of what Christ was saying in the parables of Luke. This story, he explains, is really about loyalty and what God calls us to as his Children. Though we seek approval from many people over a lifetime, it is perhaps never more powerfully sought than within family, and this is what Jesus is addressing in the life of the rich man when he says, "Sell everything you have and give to the poor, and you will have treasure in heaven. Then come, follow me."

Bailey explains that the wealth of the rich young ruler in the ancient Middle Eastern culture represented far more than just financial abundance. For the ruler, this wealth actually symbolized an enormous responsibility to his family. His wealth was the glue that held the family together and he was charged with overseeing this responsibility. When asked by Jesus to give away his wealth, the request was actually one of placing loyalty to God above loyalty to those he was expected to answer to. As a wealthy, responsible young man, Jesus stripped him of his notion of earning his way to God as "a self-assured man is faced with the radical demands of obedience."[66]

It is no wonder that Jesus said it's easier for a camel to go through an eye of a needle than for his wealthy Middle Eastern contemporaries to enter God's kingdom. Jesus was clearly placing loyalty and obedience to God far above the considerations of loyalty and approval of not only the family, but of the culture that insisted family loyalty and responsibility was unquestionable (and wealth increased the responsibility by many degrees). We rarely even consider the possibility that God may wish to challenge our family loyalties, but this parable is doing just that.

Jesus was explaining that the greater our ties in this life to possessions and family, the more difficult it is to enter God's kingdom. This kingdom is available to us right now, not at some later date when we die. The good news Jesus brought was that the kingdom of God is here, God is present with us, and the best news of all is that we are his Children. But we cannot enjoy that status if we remain tied to the loyalty and approval of our family, rather than living in the freedom of loyalty first to our Father.

I'm not even remotely suggesting that Jesus taught that we have no responsibility to people in our lives. What he is communicating, though, is that we cannot use the approval of others and our loyalty to others as a gauge for whether or not we're doing the obedient thing. Our Father is the only source for making those decisions, and obedience to him supersedes the approval from those we have attached our loyalty to. He names us Children of God, not Children of our Family. There is incredible freedom in this realization. Rather than living our lives in tune with the differing demands that surround us, and which often require things we can't live up to, God asks for obedience to only one voice and then offers his grace when we are powerless to do it in our own strength.

Our deeply loyal relationships tend to be comprised of the voices we hear first and foremost. If we go to God at all, our requests are heavy laden with the demands and expectations of those we are most loyal to. God doesn't demand that he be our only relationship, but he does expect to be our first and loudest. He created us with this intense need for human relationships, and we don't meet this need if we avoid relationships or believe errantly that somehow detaching from them will make us closer to God. In fact, the closer we become to God, the more valuable others become to us, as we gain the freedom to seek, not their approval, but honest relationships built on an understanding that we're all God's Children.

The Good Child seeks approval from a family member who wants her to take responsibility for their needs. The Child of God, understanding that the Father is perfect, that he knows our needs before we ask, and that he cares about the needs of his creation, can now say:

> "I am God's Child—I want to be obedient to my Father—I will take responsibility to love my family—promoting their dependence on me is not healthy for them—I won't take responsibility to meet needs that they need to meet in many other places—if I'm listening to, and being obedient to, my Father, who has their best interests at heart too, I don't

need my family's approval to tell me I'm
doing the right thing."

This is not an easy change in how we think about ourselves. I remember one woman saying that giving up her identity as the Good Child was like severing her left arm; the identity was so much a part of her. Being the Good Child involves a relationship with someone whose well-being you have always viewed yourself as tied to and about whom you care deeply. There is a profound sense you've not only betrayed your identity, but your family as well. The names of Self-sufficient and Perfectly Competent were tough enough for us to battle. But this name is so deeply relational, touches so piercingly at our loyalties, that the impact upon us is much more significant. The rich young ruler walked away sadly from Christ's call to obedience. So, too, might we. There is no question that the radical alteration of life that is required to deal with our anxieties has some serious costs. These costs can be felt for a long time and so anyone attempting to change this identity will have to lean heavily on the Lord to give them strength and wisdom. If we're obedient to our Father, all else will take care of itself, but to a family who expects you to seek their approval, this won't look legitimate.

This struggle is even more pronounced as we begin to deal with the dependencies that are challenged when we re-name ourselves Child of God. The Good Child has been in this relationship most of their lifetime. Dependencies are therefore powerful, but it is possible to replace them with trust in our Father as we press ahead with meeting needs appropriately. As we learn our security as Children of God, we realize he will care for those who are dependent on us, which helps us to stop trying to meet all of their needs. All we can do is model our own trust in him, but we can't convince them to try it themselves. In fact, if we take on the responsibility of helping them change, we simply reinforce dependency. We need to step out of the way, permitting the Father to do his job.

Diane was a woman who finally had the courage to tell her mom that their relationship had to make some healthy changes. This proved to be a really difficult time in her life.

> I had a clear image in my mind. My mother's anger and hurt, at what she saw as rejection, was like a dark funnel cloud, spinning wildly. I could feel its incredible pull on me. I wanted to climb into that funnel and pull her out, and somehow help her to see that her dependence on me not only hurt me, but was isolating her from the world and all it had to offer her. But I also knew that funnel would never let me free again; that if I succumbed to it, I'd enter back into my own suffocating darkness, with her clinging to me for safety. So instead, I would crawl up into my Father's lap, and hope with all my heart I was doing the right thing. I was the one person my mom wanted help from, and I was the one person who could, therefore, never be of any real help.

Diane knew her mom's dependency on her was born of so much fear that her mom would never allow anyone close to her except Diane. As long as Diane was involved, Diane's mom stayed dependent and demanding. Diane longed for her mom to turn to God and to other social contacts and friendships to meet her needs, but her mom was too afraid. Diane had become her sole source of security, and nothing Diane did or said could stop that. Diane's presence just continued to reinforce it.

Another woman, Marian, didn't have confidence in her own handling of the rift in her family that choosing to leave a dependent relationship meant for her. She consulted close friends to help her. Believing it was the Christian approach, she asked them to help her family reconcile with her. Her loving friends were hopeful for full restoration, and met with the family to suggest many ways they could be together and become restored. What Marian asked of these friends was impossible, because it failed to recognize that the family viewed reconciliation as Marian returning to the dependent relationship.

Restoration and reconciliation are Christian catchwords that we need to be wise and wary about. While worthy goals, they cannot happen within a family until everyone understands what healthy relationships look like and are committed to working toward them. It takes a great deal of sacrifice to give up the identity of Good Child, because it is nothing short of giving up dependencies that have developed over a lifetime of fear. Your sense of incredible guilt may lead you into the conversation about reconciliation long before it is even possible. If you seek to change the identity of Good Child, rejecting the expectation for family approval, and refusing to engage in dependent behavior, you can expect an extreme reaction from your family. This reaction can induce extreme guilt and a strong desire on your part to reconcile. You will need wise counsel and strong support as you seek out wisdom from God on how to handle this.

When we struggle with unhealthy dependencies, we waffle between extreme detachment and extreme attachment, because the relationships we value so much become snares we either run from or cling to. When we grasp the truth that we are Children of God, we can begin to trade our fear for his infallible security. God will not let us go, will not reject us, and will lead the way through our unknown because he knows the way. As a Child of God we experience loyalty, trust and obedience in a new way:

- Loyalty to God first.
- Trust that God will deal with our fears.
- Obedience to God only.

When we get this straight, God promises our great needs will be taken care of. "But seek first his kingdom and his righteousness, and all these things will be given to you as well."[67] Jesus says this to his listeners just after he has said "Who of you by worrying can add a single hour to your day?"[68] Now we've finally got the horse back out in front of the cart. God first, then everything will follow according to his plans, his care, and his provision.

Evelyn Underhill writes that we alternate between "an absolute and inhuman detachment and using the world of things in a childish and grasping way." Underhill goes on to explain that so much of what we try so hard to hold on to is beyond our control. Yet, we ignore this reality and carry on with the error of believing that we are better off for all that we can acquire. She concludes that a life of detachment or grasping, outcomes of attempting to possess things and people, is so much richer when replaced with dependence on God: a letting go so that we are free to enjoy it all.[69]

God calls us to a richer, deeper form of relationship, one where he, who is not passing and will not fail, is our great source of security. Out of this flows the natural development of loving relationships for our good. Our loved ones, too, have access to a loving Father, and the need for dependency shifts away from each other to security in him. We have no need for detachment or grasping, two ends of the extreme.

This is the beauty of God's work—another paradox, in which we are letting people go in order to have them. They become ours more fully when we stop grasping. God's rightful place in our lives ensures others retain their rightful place too. He will not allow them to be snatched from his hand.[70] We can let them go.

When we walk away from the name Good Child, we don't walk away from relationships. We walk away from the faulty notions of control, approval and dependency which make us anxious. God longs for us to echo David: "I will say of the Lord, 'He is my refuge and my fortress, my God, in whom I trust.'"[71] We need to live this truth, not only for ourselves, but also on behalf of those who would prefer to put that trust in us.

Anxiety at a Glance

OUR FALSE IDENTITY:

- Good Child

DETRIMENTAL THOUGHTS AND BELIEFS:

- Need for control
- Need for approval
- Unhealthy dependency

BEHAVIORAL EXAMPLES:

- Demanding the achievement of approval from a parent or the family for being the Good Child
- Attempting to control the happiness of a family member
- Attempting to meet the never-ending dependency demands of a dependent family member
- Not engaging in healthy relationships because of the Good Child's predisposition toward dependency

THE FATHER'S IDENTITY FOR US:

- Child of God

Scripture for Meditation

Psalm 139, Matthew 6:8, Matthew 6:9-13, Matthew 6:25-34, Luke 6:32-36, John 1:12-13, John 10:29-30, Romans 8:15-16, I John 3:1.

CHAPTER EIGHT

Rescuer

THE COMPLEXITY OF ANXIETY reminds me of an ocean. The ocean has many layers, the most visible of which is on the surface, where the greatest amount of light can reach it. Less and less light is visible as you go deeper into the layers of the ocean, but the waters are still teeming with life. In the same way, the symptom of anxiety lives at our surface, visible and obvious. Beneath the surface, and tougher to observe are the thoughts and beliefs we hold, and deeper still the names that drive these thoughts and beliefs, all of them fascinating, albeit dangerous. But even within the names themselves, there is depth. What I've tried to do in this book is to peer down, with each chapter, to plumb the depths of that ocean as it gets darker and more difficult to see, and in the next two chapters we're about to visit two creatures of the deep that have an enormous impact up through to the surface.

Self-sufficient is a name we can confine largely to ourselves because it's about us, but then we begin to add people to the mix with the need to have approval for being Perfectly Competent. Deeper still, we name ourselves Good Child and, rather than just needing approval, we bind the well-being of another person to us. Now I want to address this bond in even greater detail with two further names. This chapter will deal with the name Rescuer, and the next chapter, Victim. Rescuers and Victims in relationship is a bondage held together by the powers of hell. It is the most suffocating of all relationships, creating anxiety for both the Rescuer and the Victim.

I must make a huge qualifying statement before I embark on this rather treacherous ocean-side cliff. I don't want anyone to fall off, so here are the guardrails. I am never, in these next two chapters, suggesting for even one moment that we ignore the genuine victimization of anyone who is helpless to be freed from some form of oppression or aggression. When we know someone is being physically or emotionally harmed, or if we are that someone, we have a responsibility to that person and to God to take every measure within our ability to bring protection to that person and halt the demoralizing damage this can cause. Jesus is our model here. Though his mission on earth had a much deeper reach than earthly healings, he showed great compassion to those who were helpless, and he spent much of his ministry addressing those physical and mental needs that only he could.

At the same time, we must recognize there are many genuine victims in our world, those who undergo intense persecution and oppression from which they are not rescued, even despite some of man's best efforts to provide rescue. We must give them the dignity that is theirs in God's redeeming will. He defines them by his names and not as their oppression defines them. And so, too, we must not define them by their oppression, by refusing to speak the truth that even in that oppression God has given them his identity and guards closely for them what man cannot take away.

These two chapters are in no way intended to support any sort of refusal to act on behalf of the helpless when it is within your power to do so. They are also in no way encouraging you to remain in situations yourself when you are being abused by an aggressor. All of that would run counter to the greatest commandments, to love God and to love our neighbors as ourselves. So please take my words as they are meant, for those of us who have struggles in life but freedom from present victimization, recognizing genuine victimization does occur, must be acted on if possible, but does not destine someone experiencing it to be defined by their oppression.

Now that we can hopefully move on without misunderstanding, let's explore the name Rescuer. Rescuers respond to distress or their perception of possible distress in three different ways.

- Unnecessary
- Useless
- Detrimental

You'll notice not one of these methods is positive. You may be wondering why I am giving such a positive name such a bad rap. The reason is that rescue in this context is not referring to genuine need on the part of the rescued. I am not talking about a fire that someone runs into to save someone else's life, or Search and Rescue entering a sea storm to save those stranded on a ship. These are heroic efforts done on behalf of someone who is in harm's way. When I refer to the name Rescuer, I am referring to someone who doesn't know how to define real need, how to assess their own limitations to meet a perceived need, or how to respect the ability of others to figure out their own solutions.

When my husband was in high school, he and his buddies would go to one of the nearby sloughs to water-ski in summer. One of the guys couldn't swim, but he loved to get up on water-skis as long as he could launch from a shallow spot. One day they didn't have any life vests in the boat, but this guy, confident of his skiing abilities, decided he'd ski anyway. The boat pulled him up right away, but not long into the ski, he fell, flailing in the water, begging for help from those on the boat. The help he got wasn't what his desperate arm and leg thrashing expected. They calmly called to him to stand up. To his surprise he could, and the water came up to his waist.

This is a perfect image for the three mistakes of Rescuers. Unnecessary help would be to jump in and pull him to his feet. Useless help would be to jump up and down in the boat yelling to shore for someone to call 911. Detrimental help would be jumping into waist deep water to hold up the head of someone who refuses to stand (a Victim). Rescuers lack the discipline of careful assessment, and respond to the emotion of the moment, "feeling" something is bad and needs to be fixed with their help.

So what does unnecessary rescuing look like? Unfortunately I have no end of examples from my own life. I am eternally fighting this Rescue name, and though I've pretty much tamed my useless and detrimental rescuing tendencies, I hover over the unnecessary category more than I care to admit. The other night when I was at a social function talking to a man who has a new baby and is getting little sleep, I quickly jumped in with encouragement about how it gets better once they can eat a bit of rice porridge, and went on with this helpful advice until he mentioned that they had done that with their first child. I'd jumped in with unnecessary advice for a new dad who wasn't a new dad. I just wanted to make him feel better! That's the problem with a Rescuer; they never wait to see if their help is needed or wanted.

Just a few short days later, I was at a Chris Tomlin concert and early in the show, the room we were in started to get very warm. I began to get concerned. What if it got too hot for the band? Were they uncomfortable? Is somebody paying attention? I finally gave myself a shake. How is it that I need to worry about Chris Tomlin getting too warm at his own concert when he's done this at least a hundred times? Laugh at me all you want. At least I caught myself. Some of you reading this would have left your seat and gone looking for someone in charge to turn up the air conditioning.

This is unnecessary rescuing, where you and I jump in to a situation where we are neither needed nor wanted for the solution we would like to provide. It's true when our husband is hanging the Christmas lights that he's hung several years in a row, or when our friend is unhappy and we want to tell them they should feel better about what they feel bad about, or when we listen to hurting people only long enough to figure out what we think they need and then tell them. Have you ever given a string of information to someone, only to find out after you've stopped long enough to take a breath that they've known all the information for a long time? Did it escape you that even if they didn't know, this was knowledge they were most capable of discovering without your helpfulness?

So here's how the thinking goes:

> "This person has a problem to solve—I know the answer (Perfectly Competent rears her ugly head)—I will tell them what they need to know (to add a dash of control)—they will be so much better off for my helpfulness—I've just saved them from not having information they really needed."

Or:

> "This person looks like they're uncomfortable—do they need water? A sweater? The heat turned down?—I will get it for them—they'll be comfortable now."

Frankly, there are few things more annoying than someone who wants to help when their help isn't needed.

Let's move on to unhelpful rescuing, for which I have a somewhat extreme example. I once heard a presentation on British Petroleum's Macondo well which blew up in the Gulf of Mexico on April 20, 2010, with the tragic loss of 11 lives, and a huge environmental threat as vast amounts of oil leaked into the ocean. Though the presenter worked for an oil company that doesn't even operate in the States, his office was in a city where a particularly unhelpful Rescuer lived, and she somehow got his number. This lady, who explained she couldn't email BP because she had no computer and had never even surfed the internet, also explained to this man on the phone that she had a plan for how to stop the oil from escaping the blown out well. Her plan was a very simplistic lowering of some device to plug the hole, but she was confident it would work and baffled as to why no one was just getting it done.

This presenter patiently spent 45 minutes on the phone, as this woman argued her point while he tried to help her work her way through the complexity of the problem. She was unfazed by the fact that 48,000 experts were working the problem, along with 6500 ocean vessels and 110 aircraft, not to mention the 2500 miles of boom that had been set out to gather and soak up the oil on the ocean surface. She maintained her position that they just needed to give her excellent idea a try. This is classic rescue thinking—very little logic with loads of good intention.

I admit, this is an extreme example of a ridiculous departure from logic. But how many times have you given health advice when you weren't qualified, parenting advice to someone whose particular problems had never come up in your children, cheery scripture verses to someone who is beset by debilitating depression, or dire warnings about the evils of the world to teenage children who think you're as far off the current map of their life as possible?

Though mere annoyance seems to be the only problem with unnecessary and unhelpful rescuing, both of these can contribute to anxiety for the Rescuer. This is because rescuing requires a state of fretfulness and hyper-vigilance, as the Rescuer believes they have a charge they are compelled to watch over. Both of these, even when the issue is minor, place a Rescuer in an emotional state that is always one step away from anxiety. Normal events most people just work through as a part of everyday life, a Rescuer stirs the pot of their own internal juices over, ready to jump in at any moment with a perfect solution to help. We know we're in this place when the people around us have to tell us to stop fretting, let something go, or just plain lighten up.

CONTROL

A thought pattern we've mentioned before is very strongly at play in the Rescuer. Rescuers can be so controlling that they become quite annoying to others who are uninterested in being on the receiving end of their rescuing efforts. In unnecessary and unhelpful rescuing, the Rescuer may not be attempting to solve the unsolvable, but rather attempting to solve something for which their help is not required. So why on earth, we would be wise to ask, do we put so much fret and fuss into something so useless?

Some clues you're a Rescuer are that you:

- Want everyone to be happy and comfortable.
- Tend to be overly nice, overly helpful, overly apologetic.
- Tend to be the one doing most of the work in relationships.
- Can really annoy people who aren't interested in being rescued.

There is one further characteristic of Rescuers, and this characteristic pushes the scales over into the arena of detrimental. This is when Rescuers:

- Believe they are someone else's rock and protector, thinking another will be lost without them.

This is the point where we begin to move into the relationship between a Rescuer and a Victim. Jill is an example of this.

Jill was starting to experience some very odd physical symptoms. She went to the doctor and after months of testing, it was concluded a physical issue was not the problem, though she had been sure all along it was either heart disease or a brain tumor. Instead, the doctor told her that her symptoms were the result of severe anxiety attacks, and he prescribed anti-depressants with a small prescription of a sedative to get her through each attack until the anti-depressants began to work. Jill flatly refused medication, telling her doctor that if no blood test could prove her serotonin level was problematic, she couldn't accept his diagnosis. After trying natural products and lots of prayer, she still found herself with the same symptoms that originally took her to the doctor, but she remained confident in her own ability to deal effectively with the problem.

Jill's life revolved around her two kids. Her eldest, a son, was out of high school and her daughter was still in high school. She believed that they were her responsibility to protect, and though sometimes this drove her to the point of exhaustion, her deep love for them fully convinced her that they needed her constant attention. Her own home life had been void of much love. Her parents separated when she was in her teens, her father an alcoholic who rarely saw them after he left. She experienced her parent's separation with both sadness and relief. The fights were finally over, but her mother retreated into a cocoon from which she rarely emerged, and Jill finally left home when she was sixteen.

Jill had decided her kids would never experience this kind of loveless childhood. Though she too married an alcoholic who occasionally binged, her husband was kind-hearted and she managed to hide his binges (or believed she did) from the children with excuses and explanations for the sudden disappearances of their dad. Jill was an excellent pretender.

Jill's eldest, though quite capable of making a living, still lived at home with virtually no cost. He refused any post-secondary education and moved between jobs and unemployment regularly. Jill also made excuses and explanations for this behavior, and wouldn't even consider the idea of asking him to move out, believing he'd become homeless and destitute if she didn't protect him, given that he just couldn't seem to hold down a steady job and often relied on unemployment insurance.

But the top was blown off her façade of protection when she discovered that her daughter was 13 weeks pregnant. Jill didn't even realize her daughter was seeing someone, having warned her about boyfriends, citing her own childhood family as an example of relationships gone wrong. Jill was sent reeling under the shock of such a thing happening. She had always purposely limited her daughter's use of the car, planned family activities to eat up as much of the weekends as possible and regularly asked her daughter personal questions about the friends she had, as well as the activities she engaged in. Jill even snooped on her daughter's computer or read her diary just in case she wasn't getting the full story. How had she missed something this big?

Her daughter was understandably distraught and Jill jumped into supermom mode, distressed nearly beyond her own capacity, yet determined she would do everything in her power to save her daughter. She couldn't understand why God would allow such an awful thing to happen when she had worked so hard to protect her children (a new thought pattern we'll discuss later). She questioned his faithfulness because he didn't stop her daughter in those moments when Jill wasn't there. She believed her daughter's life could now be irreparably scarred, and she was fully determined to get this situation under her control.

One anxious night in bed she concocted a wild scheme that involved her daughter dropping out of school to save her the ridicule, online schooling until the baby was born, a move to another city, and raising the new grandchild as her own to protect her daughter's image. She knew it was crazy, but she couldn't think of any other way to protect her daughter from the scars that were sure to destroy her.

A wild scheme to be sure, but a Rescuer is willing to go to great lengths to "help". I've seen it get even more ridiculous. I once knew of a woman who had an affair, and then once it was over, two marriages in tatters, thought it might be a good idea for her to talk to the offended wife and let her know what her husband "needed" so they could reconcile. Rescuers are often totally clueless about how detrimental their help really is.

When dealing with her children, Jill was entirely unable to imagine their lives with pain, and she moved swiftly and exhaustingly to place herself squarely in front of any potential threat. Jill's example is a classic Rescuer thought pattern which goes like this:

> "It is my job to protect people (kids,
> friends, parents, etc.) from being hurt—
> when they are threatened with hurt,

sadness, or distress, I need to do whatever I can to relieve or reduce this, and return things to normal—If I don't rescue them, who will?"

Jill, the Rescuer, was in the business of supporting Victims. Though her daughter might decide to reject her mom's solutions, her son certainly already had accepted them. In the name of compassion and protection, Jill never allowed him to learn responsible behavior. The choices she made to protect him from life, all in the name of love, seriously interfered with his adult development; and he was most willing to engage in helplessness in order to receive her helpfulness. She believed that all she needed to do was get in his waist deep water and hold up his head when he refused to stand. Instead, they were both drowning. She'd lost her own real purpose, becoming a false solution that perpetuated his problem, and he was stuck in his choices that sabotaged maturity. She was about to do the same with her daughter and her anxiety was on a sharp rise, as she attempted to shield her daughter from the natural consequences of real choices, living in a real world.

When we name ourselves Rescuer, we attempt to solve the unsolvable by jumping into the water to hold up the head of someone whose actual need is to choose to stand. Jill's greatest joy would have been for her kids to be mature adults, making healthy choices for themselves. But rather than watch them struggle in the water until they got their legs under them, she ran for the short range solution of heads held up and lungs clear. Not only did this require hyper-vigilance as she anticipated every possible foil to her plan of safe and happy kids, she actually dismantled any hope of her long-term desire for them by refusing to let them see how awful it was to take in a breath of water.

Rescuers are among the most optimistic of people, ever believing they can help someone arrive at a destination that they have no interest in achieving for themselves. Rescuers are convinced that miraculously, through the process of being rescued, those on the receiving end will develop a desire to look after their own life.

It is entirely misplaced optimism and helpfulness, but the process is repeated over and over with the same lack of results on behalf of the Victim, and greater anxiety for the Rescuer.

Rescuers apply a lesser solution to overcome someone's refusal to do on their own what is genuinely a solution. Not only do they get anxious trying to solve the unsolvable (controlling another person's pain, choices, behaviors), but the Rescuer actually creates further problems by fostering the paralysis of another to develop the ability to deal with their own pain, choices, and behaviors. The Rescuer reinforces dependency by becoming a wall between someone they love and the real world, all the while wishing that that someone could start acting like an independent and mature adult. The Rescuer isn't only stuck between the "rock and the hard place"; they are the ones creating it.

This is a trap a Rescuer will never escape until they can give up control of another, and until they can acknowledge that rather than being a solution, they are, in fact, a large part of the problem. I can't begin to describe how terribly difficult this is, and this is in part why I said the relationship is held together by the powers of hell. So convinced is a Rescuer of another person's need of them, they find it virtually impossible to recognize that they are actually a part of the problem. If Diane in the previous chapter felt like her left arm was being severed, Jill would have felt cut in two if she had left her kids to sort out their own struggles. She believed herself responsible to shield them from pain, discomfort, embarrassment, or whatever other negative impact she perceived as a threat to their well-being.

AN OVER-DEVELOPED SENSE OF JUSTICE

This controlling behavior is further spurred on by another thought pattern which was briefly touched on when Jill became angry with God for allowing her daughter to get pregnant. I like to call this thought pattern an over-developed sense of justice because it supposes, without question, that justice equals fairness.

A Rescuer is nothing if not righteously indignant whenever both the offended and their offender aren't getting what's fair.

Has a teacher ever been unfair to your child, or a boss to your co-worker? Have you ever marched into a situation with so much boldness you surprised yourself, armed with the indignation someone you love is being treated unfairly? Rescuers are highly sensitive to unfairness, and mistakenly associate this with the justice God calls us to seek for the oppressed and the helpless. Not only are Rescuers terribly bad judges about who is actually helpless, they wrongly suppose fairness is essential to living well. And they're not afraid to correct anyone who isn't playing by those rules.

I recently heard that one of the problems on the rise for university professors is phone calls from irate parents who demand that their children get a better grade on their paper or their exam. They have many reasons why the grading is unfair to their now adult "child." Unless you want a world full of babies who can't handle reality, the best thing you can do is get out of the way and let the unfairness of life give people the opportunity to learn maturity, coping skills, and freedom from the dreaded attitude of entitlement. The demand for fairness again fosters this dependency and helplessness that disables a person from dealing with the pain, discomfort, or embarrassment that is inevitable, but which the Rescuer tries desperately to keep at bay.

Rescuers are strong-arm people. An indirect, through-the-back-door approach isn't the first thing that enters their mind when faced with unfairness. The overdeveloped sense of justice leads to thought patterns like:

> "This is wrong/unfair/unjust—I will make
> sure this is made right—I will address the
> offense on behalf of the offended—don't
> even try to get in my way."

Here is the issue with this thinking. Often, offenses can't be dealt with effectively because the offending party is not interested in our form of reconciliation. If the offender is a teacher poorly evaluating our child, they will likely not be open to our insistence that they change, nor likely will their principal. If the offending party is a family member who tells people awful things about you that aren't true, they're not likely to admit it and stop now. If the offending party is God, and he doesn't heal your terminally-ill loved one, there is little you can do to change his mind. So the Rescuer ends up fighting unfairness in life that can never be strong-armed out of its unfairness, and the Rescuer has once again found herself in the position of trying to solve the unsolvable.

These rescuing efforts can never succeed. By rescuing we continue to convince the offended that a Victim is indeed who they are. This relationship never achieves what the Rescuer seeks, which is a happier Victim. A Rescuer reinforces a Victim's identity as a Victim, as one who can never escape having been doomed to a life of unfairness and pain, when everyone else gets a better deal. This takes its natural course. A Victim sinks despairingly into hopelessness, worthlessness, bitterness and rage at never being able to escape the ravages of their pained life. A Rescuer faces the dread of realizing their efforts have been futile, feeling exhaustion at the incredible effort they keep putting in, and heart-sick about the Victim's pain. So bent are we on protection and the comfort of others, that we seem to be completely blind to the fact that all our efforts are in vain. It is our bondage.

Because of my rescuing, I lived in various states of fear for a long time. I was so bound up in trying to control outcomes and make people happy, and as these very things proved more and more elusive, I grew extremely fearful. You become a hyper-alert person, ever on edge watching for what may go wrong so you can do your best to prevent it. I was terrified by the "what ifs" that would always be outside of my ability to influence, but that I insisted were my responsibility. Deeper and deeper grew the ruts.

Rescuing is an idol, a counterfeit to the hard work of salvation. It negates the lesson Christ taught us: that salvation, genuine rescue from what will harm us, comes with the cost of personal sacrifice, both on the part of the Savior and the Saved. We've been invited to a life of "denial of self" and "losing" our life to "save it."[72] Yet, sacrifice is the four-letter word of a Rescuer, though it is a pivotal and foundational practice of the life of those who genuinely seek God. A Rescuer can't bear the thought of a Victim having to suffer and sacrifice, so a Rescuer will even go so far as to stand between God and those they protect. Rescuing itself actually becomes a form of oppression, because we insist on defining those we protect as Victims, when in reality God has so much more for all of us when his genuine rescue, his salvation, teaches us how to sacrifice.

SAVIOR

I accepted salvation from Christ in my early teens, but I never understood he was my Savior until he pulled me from the wreckage that the name Rescuer had created for me. It took a long time for me to realize and accept that life is full of pain and God's plan allows for this, sometimes insists on it out of concern for our wholeness, rather than our comfort.

I grew up in an environment familiar with religion, but not with the Christ of the Gospels. After having recently moved into a duplex on the other side of my grandmother, she one day announced it was time we go to church. I wasn't particularly keen, being a 12 year-old for one, and having experienced extreme boredom at church (thankfully only sporadically) as a child. But off we went to church, and it wasn't long before I learned things about Christ I'd never heard before. Suddenly he was no longer a baby whose story was interwoven into my Christmas fun, but someone who claimed to be God.

Initially, I accepted what I was taught in church, that I needed a Savior to take my place and pay the price for my sin or I would be doomed to eternity without God. I didn't understand what this really meant, but I accepted it as a progression in my understanding of the God I had always believed in. I viewed this salvation as something spiritual and unearthly, so the fact that it didn't entirely make sense wasn't really an issue. I accepted that this salvation took place somewhere in the heavenly realm where a cosmic justice must occur, and it little affected me, other than inviting me into the culture and community of Christian faith. Frankly, I thought Christians were all a bit weird, but they were nice, and my grandma was unrelenting.

Later, as I grew in my faith and in my church experience, I began to take righteousness very seriously, so much so, that strict fundamental teachings influenced me quite heavily. I began to take on the responsibility for the fruits of salvation: a good, clean, and wholesome life. I began to travel down the road many who turn to faith find themselves on. I became a bit of an expert in the law.

One of the great outcomes of my crash with anxiety was the revelation, as I got on the path of healing, that salvation is far more than a ticket to eternal life. When God refers to himself as our Savior, he gives definition to the name. He tells us that as Savior he is our shield and refuge.[73] He delivers us from guilt[74], and daily bears our burdens.[75] He saves and defends us when we cry out because of our oppressors, rescuing us[76], with the clear explanation that apart from him there is no savior.[77] Salvation is an overarching plan that unfolds over time as we allow God's kingdom to live within us on a daily basis, and then as a salvation that somehow reaches out to all on the earth when "every knee will bow."[78] We don't fully grasp salvation now, but we wait in expectation that he has saved us from the finality of death, that one day in immortality we will know all the benefits of our Savior when we rest with him in our eternal dwelling. But in this life, his salvation is very much at work as he delivers us, rescues us, defends us, and daily bears our burdens with us. These benefits are real, as we learn to trust him in all circumstances, allowing him to do what only he can do to bring about the salvation we need in our moments right here and now. I had no idea of my own need of salvation from a troubled mind that was never at rest in the security of Christ.

Sacrifice has so long, in the tradition of my faith, been something that is offered to God as way of making us clean from our sins, that I for many years saw Christ's death on the cross only in this light. But the truth of what Jesus did in the offering of himself has a far greater reach. Jesus died because he refused to give up on his insistence that God's Kingdom was current, that God was in charge, and that everyone, as they were, could enter: no personal righteousness, political strength, gender or race could earn them entrance or hold them back. The good news was that those who wanted it could have it freely, a gift offered in the grace of God, because all people were equal under his kingdom rule.

When the Word, who spoke creation into existence, decided to enter our world as a human, he came at a time when his people (Israel) had hopelessly derailed from their commission to be a light to all nations.[79] God's plan for his people was to raise them up in order to draw all nations to himself, but they had a long history of dismal failure. And their current attempts weren't any more successful. The nationalist zealots, of whom Judas was one, wanted to overthrow the government and take back their land. The religious elite who were charged with shepherding the flock, were oppressing those poor lost sheep with rules and laws that kept God at a distance, not only from the flock, but most certainly from the surrounding nations that watched them put shackles of legalism on their people. Enter the Word Incarnate: "The Lord will lay bare his holy arm in the sight of all the nations, and all the ends of the earth will see the salvation of our God."[80] He had come to do the work God had planned from the very beginning of this nation. "Be still and know that I am God. I will be exalted among the nations; I will be exalted in the earth."[81]

But, what Jesus came to do was more than irritating to the agenda of the religious elite and the nationalistic hope of the zealots. He began his ministry with these words from Isaiah 61:1-2 "The Spirit of the Lord is on me, because he has anointed me to preach good news to the poor. He has sent me to proclaim freedom for the prisoners and recovery of sight of the blind, to release the oppressed, to proclaim the year of the Lord's favor." Luke 4:23-30 then goes on to reveal Christ's first assault on the aims of his people when he reminded them that God sent Elijah and Elisha to meet the needs of Gentiles rather than Jews. This enraged them, because they had lost their bearings and become entirely inwardly focused, refusing to accept that their responsibility was to draw more than just the Jewish nation to God.

Our Savior proclaimed freedom and recovery of sight by telling his people that the kingdom was present, with them right now, and that the kingdom was received through the grace of a loving God, not through merit and religious practice, and not through power and government takeovers. He didn't come to rescue his people by taking control and enacting social justice; he came to save his people by preaching the gospel of grace, the extreme of a total dependence on God to live in a world that does not, even in its most religious moments, reflect the beauty of God. He called his people to be that beauty, and went to his death re-telling them the story of grace and mercy, when the Pharisees wanted to hold their feet to the fire of earning their way and the zealots wanted to overthrow Rome.

Jesus wouldn't quit with his rendition of God's real story that the Israelites had long forgotten. He remained obedient to God regardless of the cost, a cost which he understood very well. We have an excellent example of how Jesus dealt with the rescuing mentality in Matt. 16:21-23. He, the Son of God, who had the armies of heaven at his disposal, told his disciples about the death he was about to submit himself to, and a rescuing Peter declared with authority, "This shall never happen to you!" And how did Jesus respond? He rejected Peter's stance and called him a stumbling block because he did not have in mind the things of God.

How many times have Rescuers been a stumbling block to someone because they stood in the way of what God had in mind?

Jill caused her children to stumble about in immaturity because she kept getting in the way of God's best for them. Rescuers who insist on being someone's rock never get out of the way for God to do that job instead. Rescuers want life to be fair, but Jesus, directly after he rebuked Peter for being a Rescuer, told his disciples, "If anyone would come after me, he must deny himself and take up his cross and follow me. For whoever wants to save his life will lose it, but whoever loses his life for me will find it." (Verses 24-25) Sacrifice is what he calls us to, and sacrifice is exactly what a Rescuer tries to interfere with.

The Savior came to sacrifice himself, and as the recipients of the gift he gave, we need to learn something about what sacrifice does for us, in us, and to us when we are willing to engage in it ourselves.

I will attempt an allegory to illustrate how sacrifice achieves what rescuing cannot.

There were two young sisters who lived by the sea. They were very close in age and were each other's greatest companions. They would play in the sand day after day, pretending to sail the seas on various boats and rafts crafted from driftwood, built on the safety of the shore. But their imaginations knew no bounds. Together they had many adventures and their simple life pleased them. As they matured and grew closer to adulthood, the youngest sister grew more serious and brooding, most obviously on the dark and rainy days of winter, end over end dreariness penetrating her soul. The eldest sister, so concerned for her youngest, would dance, sing, and play high-spirited games to try and entice her young sister out of her dark places.

The sisters lived near a village full of high peaked, pastel-colored houses set in the rocks overlooking the sea. The eldest sister would often visit the village, making friends who would occasionally come home with her, and she hoped this would cheer her sister. However, this only served to frighten her younger sister, afraid that they would not like her as much as her older sister, and afraid too of the possibility that they could steal her sister away.

On one such visit to the village to find an idea to cheer her sister, the eldest sister met a very handsome man. After many more visits to the village, this man stole her heart and soon became her betrothed. Overjoyed, she danced home one day from the village, only to see her sister on the beach, waiting for her return. Her joy vanished as she anticipated her young sister's reaction to the news she would soon go to marry her Lover and live in the village.

The reaction was far worse than the eldest had imagined. Over the course of many days and weeks, the youngest sister became more and more enraged at the betrayal she felt from her eldest sister, and she began to tell her sister "I hate you!" What she really meant, though, was "Don't leave me!" The eldest sister tried to no avail to explain that, though things would change, her love would not change for the youngest sister. The eldest sister's heart ached, knowing the things that had to change would bring her sister great pain. She knew that meeting her own needs of love would ensure her sister's misery.

A surprising thing, unexpected and terrible, happened out of the youngest sister's misery. Once terrified of the village, the youngest sister in her distraught state sought out the villagers for solace. In her deep turmoil, she imagined all kinds of terrible things that her older sister had done to her, none of them real, but all more than real to the youngest sister because of the searing pain she felt in her heart. Soon, the villagers became angry with the eldest sister and chided her when they saw her on the street, demanding she make right the terrible wrongs she had done.

The eldest sister was so stunned by the accusations, she ran from the village speechless. She ran straight to her Lover and in tears of pain and anger, poured out her woes to him and set out her plan for righting this wrong. But her Lover, with great love and tenderness, placed his finger on her mouth and told her she must not do this. Instead, he said, she must be silent in the face of the accusations. For to defend herself would be to accuse her sister, which would isolate her sister from the villagers, destroy her sister's credibility, doing nothing for her own. He promised her that through all that would come, he would stand by her and protect her from harm.

Out of deep trust in her Lover, the eldest sister did as he requested. It was a painful time, but he stood by her side through it all as he promised. She became the scorn of the village and regularly wept in the arms of her Lover. The villagers, sensing the love and care the youngest sister needed in her obvious and open pain, rallied around her and she grew close to many of them. Over time she found her life, for the first time, rich with relationships. It soon became evident that these were real relationships that met many more needs than her eldest sister could ever meet.

What happened to the eldest sister was not inconsequential either. The energy she would have used to defend herself she now put into trying to understand why her beloved sister would speak such awful things about her. She began to discover in herself a genuine love and care for her sister, one that wasn't about rescuing her from her dark places, but one that understood the brokenness of the youngest sister that could never be reached by the eldest being her rock and fortress. The eldest finally learned how to love her young sister in the freedom from guilt and duty, exchanged for love for the sake of love alone. She had let her sister go, only to find that greater love came of it. She also was able to give her young sister the freedom to accept that love or reject it, letting go of control of how her sister reacted.

Over the course of time it became clear that the village was no place for them to stay, so the eldest and her Lover left. On sad days, when she mourned the loss of her youngest sister, her Lover reminded her that through the sacrifice of her own reputation, she had done more for her young sister than when she was trying to rescue her by being her constant companion.

Jesus is the Lover of our souls. His ministry was full of paradoxes and contradictions to our common sense, yet with wonderfully profound results. He rejected the control-taking religious elite who felt they could take their destiny with God into their own legalistic hands and gain access through personal merit. He rejected the zealots who wanted to take Rome by storm and conquer their oppressors. Both of these groups represent the thoughts of a Rescuer: control and an overdeveloped sense of justice. Instead, he, the very Word who spoke creation into being, was born in a stable, raised in poverty, taught that the first would be last and the last, first, and called us to deny self and lose our life to save it. He then died a horrifying death that he could have avoided but chose instead to silently endure, without defense. He knew more was to be gained through sacrifice than through the "rescuing" efforts of the Pharisees and zealots.

SAVED

God may call Jill to sacrifice her kids by releasing them to the realities of life. He may tell her they belong to him, not her, that all her attempts to make them happy have been futile, and that her constant lecturing and preaching about the evils of this world have done nothing to rescue her daughter. The truth is that there is more to be gained with God walking through her daughter's pain with her, than with Jill running out in front leading all the blocking to potential pain. His is a plan for salvation, not rescue. Rescue is a poor substitute for genuine salvation.

Here is the paradox of Jesus' ministry. We are saved through sacrifice, not through tough tactics and behaviors that control outcomes. This image of sacrifice wasn't just for Jesus' "there and then" in Jerusalem, but for our "here and now" wherever we find ourselves. Sacrifice saves us. It saves us from the blindness of our sense of control over others (that we never had) and the bondage of dependencies we foster but that only provide a counterfeit love born of isolation and fear, rather than freedom and openness to life. Sacrifice frees us from the attitude of entitlement by revealing to us the beauty of what lies beyond getting what we think we deserve. It trains us in maturity, builds our coping mechanisms, strengthens us in the inner parts of our being, and is a mystery at work to save us from the shells of ourselves that we become when we live in avoidance of it.

"But wait", you say, "I'm not afraid to give of myself, to sacrifice myself on behalf of another. What you describe as rescuing is actually me sacrificing myself for another. I'm willing to be treated unfairly, I'm not afraid to hurt, to be mocked, to give of myself for the benefit of others, to endure the natural consequences of my mistakes." Then my question to you is this. Why aren't you able to let those you try to rescue do exactly the same thing? Is it because you have defined yourself as stronger, as the Rescuer, and them as weaker, as Victims?

Jesus, when naming us Saved, calls us to a life which will involve sacrifice. When we try to shield those we want to rescue from this very thing, we're interfering with the work of salvation. For Jesus, if obedience to God's call on his life meant death, even death on a cross[82], he would obey nonetheless. Philippians 2 tell us the attitude that we need.

"Your attitude should be the same as that of Christ Jesus: Who being in very nature God, did not consider equality with God something to be grasped, but made himself nothing, taking the very nature of a servant, being made in human likeness. And being found in appearance as a man, he humbled himself." (Verses 5-8)

Jesus was neither a Rescuer nor a Victim. He modeled sacrifice to us so we could grasp what it means to come out the other side of obedience with a gift that surpasses anything we could control. Our Savior didn't talk about human rights, being fair, and taking charge. He spoke of obedience and humility, not the least ashamed to be born in obscurity in a stable.

Our Savior taught us that a rescue isn't what we need. He hasn't rescued us from inequality, disease, hunger, broken hearts, and a myriad of other plagues that besiege the human race. He called us blessed when we are poor in spirit, meek, hungry for righteousness, merciful, pure in heart, peacemakers, and persecuted. We are Saved, our bondage broken, as we learn to love through the sacrifices that life calls us to.

This isn't cheap sacrifice, the kind that we decide upon and then go about sacrificing to prove something to God or ourselves. Genuine sacrifice doesn't come from our decision to offer something up to God, yet again relying on self to do the impressing. Genuine sacrifice happens out of opportunities that God takes to ask something of us when that something runs totally counter to what we want to do. Self-inflicted sacrifice probably won't kill you, but it misses the point. God decides what we need, and then he calls us to give up or accept something that will do the job.

Prior to this chapter, I haven't talked a great deal about the sacrifices involved in a healing journey out of anxiety. But, I certainly believe that healing cannot take place apart from learning how to sacrifice, and learning how to do that well. So often we interpret salvation as our guarantee that we'll have eternal life. End of story. Then the rest is up to us. We have to keep ourselves on the narrow path, attend church every week, and submit to whatever set of rules our particular denomination defines necessary for pure living. But salvation, the gift of being the Saved, is so much richer, mysterious, and complex.

Christ told us he came to set the captives free.[83] This freedom wasn't a physical one, where the Roman government suddenly vanished and was replaced with God's rule. This was a spiritual freedom Christ referred to, one that had a much broader perspective than mere physical freedom. This was the freedom of mind and spirit, an illumination of truth in this life, as well as the next, so that the burdens of this world were bathed in the light of eternity and the unfaltering love of God.

God wasn't taking away the struggles and oppression of this world; he was opening our minds to the understanding that this life cannot oppress that which we decide to give to him for safe-keeping. That part of us that lives in our spiritual selves, much deeper and more concrete than the flesh and blood that lets us down, is protected by our Savior. He provides a defense and rescue that can be experienced within, something no one can take away, cut out, or kill. That part of us can be given to our Savior and he will shield us, defend us, protect us, and rescue us.

> "It is for freedom that Christ has set us
> free. Stand firm, then, and do not let
> yourselves be burdened again by a yoke
> of slavery."[84]

God values our freedom so much that he freed us for the sake of freedom. It is a double emphasis for a reason. Our freedom is of great value to him. But this freedom does not manifest itself in obvious ways. We see people suffer with no apparent salvation from their bondage. We observe people living with sin and no apparent interest in living differently. This starts to get very uncomfortable for us. This enormous discomfort can lead to a decision to step in and do something, something which feels like salvation but only ends up as interference.

Salvation is about learning to suffer well. "We also rejoice in our sufferings, because we know that suffering produces perseverance; perseverance, character; and character, hope."[85] And this is because suffering is an inevitable part of life. We're not dealing with the possibility that there will be sacrifices to be made in life. We're dealing with the reality that life will lead us to face great difficulties. It will happen, regardless of our attempts to thwart it.

Jesus invites us to live in submission, to let go of our lives and our comfort, and to let God ask of us what he will, giving us comfort or sacrifice, wealth or poverty, success in a moment or failure in many. The invitation to die to self isn't for the purpose of pain, but for the purpose of revealing the "so much more" that God has to offer us in a life lived without grasping. And so, the Rescuers of Jesus' earthly ministry, the Pharisees and the political zealots, would have nothing to do with him.

Anxiety at a Glance

OUR FALSE IDENTITY:

- Rescuer

DETRIMENTAL THOUGHTS AND BELIEFS:

- Need for control
- An over-developed sense of justice

BEHAVIORAL EXAMPLES:

- Engaging in unnecessary, unhelpful or detrimental "rescuing"
- Attempting to control circumstances on behalf of someone who is capable of addressing their own needs, even if they refuse this responsibility

THE SAVIOR'S IDENTITY FOR US:

- Saved

Scripture for Meditation

Job 40:9-14, Psalm 42, Psalm 51:17, Psalm 107:1-22, Psalm 146:3-4, Isaiah 30:15-18, Isaiah 46:4-13, Matthew 16:21-25, Romans 12:1, Philippians 2:5-11, Hebrews 2:10.

CHAPTER NINE

Victim

IN HIS BOOK *WHY Zebras Don't Get Ulcers*, Robert Sapolsky demonstrates something fascinating about the relationship of predictability and control to stress in animals. He explains that when rats are subjected to electrical shocks over which they have no control and which they cannot predict, rather than learning how to cope, they develop what is called "learned helplessness."

> One might wonder whether the helplessness is induced by the physical stress of receiving the shocks or, instead, the psychological stressor of having no control over or capacity to predict the shocks. It is the latter....
> Animals with learned helplessness also have a cognitive problem, something awry with how they perceive the world and think about it. When they do make the rare coping response, they can't tell whether it works or not....By all logic, that rat should have learned, "When I am getting shocked, there is absolutely nothing I can do, and that feels terrible, but it isn't the whole world; it isn't true for everything." Instead, it has learned, "There is nothing I can do. Ever." Even when control and mastery are potentially

made available to it, the rat cannot perceive them.[86]

Sapolsky then goes on to explain that learned helplessness can be induced in humans rather easily, but is very dependent on personality. Those who have an "internalized locus of control" or a sense of their own personal mastery, are far less likely to be susceptible to learned helplessness than those who have an "externalized" view, who tend "to attribute outcomes to chance and luck", which appears to make them "far more vulnerable to learned helplessness."[87]

But what do rats have to do with our anxiety? Some anxious people will tell you that they do at times feel like life is hopeless, and they will go on to describe their world in the external locus of control fashion Sapolsky describes. There are times in the life of an anxious person when all effort to exert control and fix problems leads us to a sense of the futility of our efforts, and we feel like we're a victim of circumstances rather than an active participant in life. We can begin to believe that, regardless of what we do, life is going to let us down. It is in these times we slip into a name that drags us into the undertow of despair. The name is Victim.

Victim has the appearance of a legitimate name when you listen to the Victim's story. It is easy to become convinced that life has dealt them some hard blows and to pity them the stuck places they are in. While Rescuers are the "internal locus of control" people, who believe in their own ability to overcome obstacles, Victims become people who have given up, assigning control over to someone or something over which they can exert no control, and from which they receive whimsical, even cruel pain. Like the rats in the study, they believe unquestionably that there is nothing they can do. Ever.

Victims are the perfect partner for Rescuers, each reinforcing one another's identity. Both believe that fundamentally life should be controllable and predictable. Rescuers set out to make this a reality and Victims despair because it isn't. This despair drives the Rescuer to mobilize their "internal locus of control" belief, looking for ways to right the wrongs done to the Victim. The Victim, receiving attention for the wrongs done, is reinforced as a Victim of unfairness by the Rescuer who insists that they've been unfairly treated and that this must be solved. Victims also receive reinforcement from Rescuers in their belief that they are helpless—that someone external to them controls their destiny. When the Rescuer fails to bring about adequate "fairness", this only further reinforces a Victim's identity.

Not unlike rats, we look to the world to be controllable and predictable. When we feel out of control and unable to predict what will happen next, we become anxious. For a Victim, anxiety can be coupled with the learned helplessness state Sapolsky talks about.

Lynette was someone I met with only briefly. She was looking for someone who could understand her struggle with anxiety because it had been a lifelong demon for her, and when we first met she made it clear she doubted she would ever be free of it. She was clearly resigned, and as she spoke it became obvious that more than anxiety stalked her life. She also lived under a cloud of depression that, like anxiety, had been an intermittent lifelong battle.

Lynette described God to me. "He is", she said, "the big clockmaker in the sky, who wound up the world and now sits back and watches it unfold." His interest in her was nothing more than observation, unless she failed him, and then his interest was aroused. At this point, he could suddenly be counted on to punish her failure. Hers was an ugly god, demanding much and giving little. She asked me what I thought the point of talking about anxiety was, given that her god would never change and she would forever be doomed to the futility of trying to squeeze one bit of compassion from this largely disinterested, and sometimes dangerous, deity. Her god was a sociopath, an emotionless void, lacking empathy or concern for this woman who called herself one of the faithful—faithfulness to her meaning a life of religious observance fraught with fear. She was convinced she would always be unworthy in his eyes, regardless of the perfection she continually demanded of herself.

I remember well an image of myself when I first began my ascent out of anxiety. I was looking down from the rafters onto the floor of a theatre stage. The floors of the stage were boards, rough and uneven, and the stage itself was void of any set except for a metal walled cage, four-sided with the roof missing. The lighting was bright enough, but the color of the room was mostly a muted brown, like a sepia photograph.

This play's set reeked of sadness and fear, and then, from my vantage point in the rafters, I looked inside the metal cage. In it, sitting on the floor in a puddle of tears, was me. Though there was a door out, I was locked inside and I was crying because I was hopelessly confined with no escape. As this image penetrated my mind, it was as if a camera lens suddenly zoomed in on my hand, clasp tightly around something I appeared oblivious to. Inside that hand was the key to the door, and I was instantly jolted from the image out into my own real life. I lived a life steered by the fear of unpredictability and loss of control. In that instant, I knew my life's key had always been in my own hand and I'd refused myself freedom. God had so much more for me than the life of names I'd been living. The desperate attempts to control outcomes and keep danger at bay had confined me to a prison of my own making.

Lynette lived in sepia. She had her hand wrapped tightly around the key of her prison and she refused to let it go for even a second, but her grip was somewhat different than mine. While I had lived always vigilant, trying to control outcomes, Lynette had succumbed to giving up on trying any longer. Any efforts at gaining control and mastery over outcomes in her world had failed. She was convinced that she was a casualty of a detached and demanding god, and she was absolutely right. Her god was an idol named Victim, and she was bent on serving that name.

Lynette married young, had two children early in the marriage, and then was left to raise them alone when her husband suddenly left town with his secretary. Educated as a teacher, she returned to work and committed herself to raising her children. But this was a frightening time for Lynette, and she began to experience serious bouts of panic, particularly when she thought about her future alone with her two kids. She felt life had been her enemy from this point on, and she had begun then to dread what she referred to as the "many boogey men" she expected around every corner.

Now, years later, with two grown children, Lynette recounted all the difficulties in her life. She was abandoned, and felt nothing but hatred for her former husband. She didn't cultivate social relationships after he left, focusing her efforts on the kids, and found life lonely, though the thought of engaging in social contacts seemed dangerous. She had never enjoyed people, always believing they would in the end fail her. She had a long list of proof of this: a principal who sided against her with the other "less than adequate" teachers in her place of employment, one ungrateful son who moved to Australia to get to know his dad, and most of all, the big clock maker in the sky who cared little for the unfairness of all her suffering.

Her only source of real comfort had been her mom, who she referred to as her "safe harbor", but her mom had suffered a fatal heart attack three years earlier. That was a crushing loss for Lynette.

All five of the thought patterns are at the core of the name Victim: control, approval, blame, dependency, and an over-developed sense of justice. Lynette is an illustration of this. Because all of the thought patterns seem to converge on this one name, it is a very difficult identity to throw off. This powerful name has debilitating effects on the life of anyone who chooses to wear it.

For clarity, we'll look at the thought patterns in the order of blame, justice, approval, dependency and control, as they build on one another. These thought patterns as they relate to the name Victim have strong ties to the names Self-sufficient and Perfectly Competent.

Lynette carried both the names of Self-sufficient and Perfectly Competent. When bearers of these names fail to live up to them, they lose their confidence, though still insisting that they must measure up to the demands these names require. This is when we bump up against the opposite sides of the coin of pride: arrogance and insecurity, when we measure up and when we don't, both a result of pride that demands self has to earn merit. This is our ceaseless endeavor as humans to prove we can do it ourselves.

Lynette believed she had failed at her merit-earning endeavors. She cringed to admit it, but when she started to look past her fierce anger at her ex-husband, former principal, and son that moved away, she was terrified that she might have to take some responsibility for failure. Perhaps she had created so many waves at work, she'd become a problem employee. Perhaps her husband recognized in her something she had always feared—that she was worthy of only rejection. Perhaps her son wished she hadn't been the parent who raised him. These images of potential failure were just too painful. The sense of shame was so great that she absolutely fought against the terrifying thought that she hadn't achieved what the names Self-sufficient (as a single mother) and Perfectly Competent (as a teacher and a wife) demanded of her. To shield herself from the pain, blame became her outlet.

BLAME

In order to seek vindication for her sense of failure, Lynette had convinced herself she was powerless and unable:
"I can't help it, life is too hard, the world
is cruel, and I'm too weak."
When it looked to her like her life was in a serious mess, she managed to avoid addressing her own failure (whether real or imagined) by insisting that she was a Victim of someone else's failure. Her ex, principal, and son became demons, not men, deserving of venom and hostility.

The common foible of black and white thinking dogs the life of a Victim. People become either good or bad, so there was no room for the possibility that these men might have good and bad attributes. For Lynette, they were evil and had become her proof point that she did not bear the responsibility for any of her problems related to them. They were her oppressors and abusers, the cause of her problems. This thinking provided an outlet for not living up to the Self-sufficient and Perfectly Competent standards that Lynette refused to let go.

AN OVER-DEVELOPED SENSE OF JUSTICE

You can't have blame without the insistence that justice must be served. The Victim, defining justice as fairness, sets out to prove that they have been treated unfairly, that life hasn't dealt them a fair hand. Lynette took great offense at everyone in her life that had hurt her and she kept a list of accounts of this hurt. Lynette was hostile about this, enraged at the unfairness, and sometimes the lid came off and she lashed out in a tirade of hostility and bitterness. Anyone aware of the tirade or the occasional outbursts of rage had to be helped, she believed, to recognize that she couldn't stop herself. What had happened to her brought this out in her, and she was in need of pity for the unfairness of it all. Victims work hard to point out that life isn't fair to them and that justice has been denied them.

> "Life should be fair, it isn't for me, and
> until you see that I must keep my misery
> on display."

It wasn't enough that Lynette had convinced herself of these things. She also needed to convey these "truths" to others. These "truths" were formed after days, months, maybe even years of rolling thoughts around without the benefit of an outside perspective. Alone in the mind of the Victim, the thoughts take on a reality of their own. The realities of an incident get lost in the interpretation necessary for the Victim to prove that they are blameless and that life isn't fair. This has gone on for so long that the Victim sincerely believes their version of "truth."

APPROVAL

The Victim must convince others of the reality they've come to believe in order to receive approval for the role they've taken on. Believing that everyone demands self-sufficiency and perfect competence, the Victim fears they'll be viewed poorly for not measuring up. Therefore, the Victim has to work hard to prove her "right" to her current state by proving she is a Victim of another's behavior and that life is not fair. As long as Lynette could convey this "truth" to others, she felt she could receive approval from them. This became her substitute for approval for achievement, and helped Lynette bear her own failure, because now she was not held responsible for it.

When you despise failure, Victim is a tempting name to slip on. Pity may not be the most desirable response of approval that you can get for your mistakes, but if you can convince people of two things: you aren't responsible because you're a Victim, and you're a Victim at the hands of unfairness in life, this feels better than a full-blown acceptance of responsibility for what you couldn't achieve. The wicked slave masters remain Perfectly Competent and Self-sufficient, ever demanding that which we can't produce and shaming us when we fail, pushing us to look for any relief we can find.

DEPENDENCY

Further relief and reinforcement for the Victim is a Rescuer, someone who will console the Victim and reinforce their name by reassuring them through rescuing efforts that this is indeed who they are. These relationships develop into strong ties of dependency. Sadly, the pity and attention of a Rescuer is the meager meal of a Victim. Sometimes it is their only meal because the behaviors of dependency have driven away most everyone else. Some Victims can be challenging personalities. Their survival has been so tightly bound to interpreting other's behavior as the justification for their own, that they habitually criticize and judge even those who pose no threat to them. Not good party behavior, and sensing this, they often reject the party before they can be rejected.

Returning to the five fears of dependency in chapter seven, we bump up against the entire set of hurdles a Victim must deal with.

1. Fear of rejection.
2. Fear of aloneness.
3. Fear of the unknown.
4. Fear of confronting problems head-on.
5. Fear of being revealed/discovered.

Dependency is treacherous because it becomes the counterfeit for meeting legitimate social, emotional, etc. needs that the Victim is terrified will go unmet if that one Rescuer, that one rock they can always count on, is no longer there. This was a large part of Lynette's battle to deal with the loss of her mother. She was the one person who really understood how victimized by life Lynette was. She could be counted on to support Lynette's version of the truth and reinforce it by taking on the responsibility of trying to make Lynette happy. In her dependent relationship, Lynette had some control over getting her needs met, but her mother's death stripped her of control. She now felt adrift, having no one who understood her like her mother did, yet still seeking out a similar relationship to fill that need.

CONTROL

This leads to the final thought pattern of the Victim: control. The Victim must engage in various methods of control to ensure that this dependent relationship remains intact. The relationship between Rescuer and Victim is always at risk if the Victim fails to be victimized. Victims must continually carry on the work of convincing their Rescuer that they are a Victim, creating elaborate interpretations of life events that inevitably wind up with them on the bottom, wounded. Manipulation becomes a big part of this effort: sometimes using guilt, sometimes pity and sometimes threats to ensure the Rescuer stays close, protective, and keeps trying to fill up the Victim's emptiness. The danger of loss of a Rescuer creates a great deal of anxiety for the Victim. A Victim is always on guard for rejection or loss because life is viewed as eternally unfair.

My husband tells the story of the false face. It is one of his favorites and it depicts so clearly what happens to us when we fall prey to this name. A false face is a mask that we wear in front of others so they can't see who we really are. We know we aren't perfect, but we can't bear this truth, so we put up the mask to hide our real selves. The problem is that when we put up that false face, love can never get through to the real us. If someone shows us love, deep down we know they only love that part of us we've revealed, in this case, the Victim. If love is withdrawn, we suspect they've looked past the mask to see the deepest parts of us. We're convinced those parts are unlovable because we ourselves hate them so much. So we have to work hard to keep the mask of Victim up because it provides the cover we need. As long as it works, how could our Rescuer, or even God, not take pity on us?

The Victim is convinced that any difficult situation is another event in the long line of proof that they're powerless and the world is out to get them. Unwilling to accept problems as a legitimate part of life, the Victim must find someone to blame, giving away responsibility as well as the solution to someone else. A Victim is convinced that they act the way they do because of the power someone else holds over them, oppressing them or refusing to rescue them. Enter the Rescuer, stage right, ready to be the solution-giver. This is his time to shine, armed with control and an overdeveloped sense of justice, and most certainly, a "can-do" attitude. A Victim behaves in self-destructive or relationship damaging ways out of the belief that they have no other choice given the oppression they are under. A Rescuer supplies the vindication for the Victim's bad choices by reinforcing that they can't prevent their own response and so need a good and solid rescue. While the Rescuer tries to control the Victim's happiness, the Victim tries to control the involvement of the Rescuer with pity, wounded withdrawal, guilt manipulation, and even hostility when the relationship feels at risk.

Giselle's mom was a Victim. A wounded woman, she entered marriage to a wounded man. Some of us are blessed to escape life's lessons unscathed, but many of us get wounds. And we bring them into our relationships in the hopes that this other wounded person will be able to make us better. But that doesn't usually happen. Instead, the woundedness leads to bad relational interactions that compound the wounds.

When Giselle's dad was insensitive and hurtful out of his own wounded place, Giselle's mom felt nothing but rejection, lashing out in vicious anger at him. He then disengaged from her to avoid the chaos, and her sense of rejection found a toehold. As the cycle was repeated, the wounds compounded further and the damaging behavior was reinforced.

Giselle grew up watching this mess and said to herself, "Someone has got to do something." So Giselle became her mother's Rescuer, defending her by agreeing that her mom was a Victim of her dad's behavior, trying to soothe the wounds by listening, agreeing, taking sides and generally reinforcing how victimized and rejected her mom felt. To leave her mom to work out her problems with her dad would have appeared to Giselle to be further rejection and victimization of her mom. Giselle may have even believed that her mom couldn't possibly survive without her. Giselle couldn't leave the stage—ever. And Giselle's mom's grip on her own prison key got tighter and tighter.

The darkness and despair of powerlessness and rejection is utterly engulfing. It becomes a prison into which Victims lock themselves. They won't acknowledge that imperfection is part of the human condition, that pain exists alongside the goodness and wholeness of God's kingdom on earth, that strife and calamity are inevitable, and that we are each responsible to take our needs seriously and have them legitimately met in obedience to God.

We are seductively wooed to walk into our prison and take the key with us, locking the door from the inside.

There are at least three reasons for this seduction. The first is that when we call ourselves powerless, a miracle happens. All those things we've done, bad habits that have forged caverns in our lives, relationships we've destroyed out of selfishness and sin, can be absolved simply by denying that they were ever something we bore some responsibility for. We are pardoned of responsibility for flawed behavior because we're actually a Victim of circumstances. Preferring to lie to ourselves about who we've been, we erect a prison that hides the truth about us. We learn how to pretend. We choose to see problems in life as evidence that we are a helpless Victim who has been taken advantage of and will continue to be taken advantage of.

The second reason for choosing the name Victim is its delicious flavor, an enjoyable torment that can relish pointing an accusing finger. Too strong you say? I don't think so. One of the pleasures of this name is the freedom to judge, accuse, and twist the actions and words of the oppressor, whoever that happens to be. Victims have a black and white attitude toward others. You either fall into the camp of good or evil, and if you're in the latter, a Victim enjoys the liberty of painting your every move with a blackened brush.

The third reason is the rather strange pleasure in self-pity that is actually self-harm. Victims look for oppression in the actions of another for the very odd comfort of reinforcing their own status as Victim. There is pleasure in the pain of their suffering; it is a masochistic self-pity.

The mind-set required to root out and uncover wrongs done by others means negativity must be nurtured. A negative, judgmental and suspicious focus is fundamental to the process. Judgmental, critical, and morose thinking become a regular part of a Victim's daily life. If grace for their fallibility is something they can't accept, it certainly isn't something they can offer to others. This lack of grace is only bearable as long as their own fallibility is masked while other's is highlighted. And it is precisely through the highlighting that they are most able to mask their own. The cycle becomes closed in on itself.

Victims live with suffocating fear. They must rely on their ability to convince others of the injustices done to them, in order to gain approval for behavior entirely unacceptable to them, using means that can potentially drive people away from them, and all while anticipating rejection that they are sure is due them. I can't think of a more poignant illustration of the "rock and the hard place."

The only escape is for the Victim to acknowledge personal fallibility and absolute dependence on grace—a terrifying and questionable prospect. An entire worldview of black and white, good and bad has to be discarded and replaced with something so shockingly beautiful it just can't possibly be true, and so shockingly unfair it just isn't fair. We have a God who is able to lift us, as well as those who have wronged us, up out of our mess and redeem it all. He is our Redeemer.

REDEEMER

It's tough to choose a name for God that I love most. But this name, Redeemer, reveals a beauty in God that stuns me, and once I'm shaken from the disbelief of it all, fills my heart to brimming over with gratitude. To redeem is to buy back, recover ownership of, and to restore something to its former place. It's a beautiful representation of yet another paradox of faith. The very thing that brings us such great good (redemption) is the bondage that made the purchase necessary. Redemption can only occur where there is brokenness and bondage.

Scripture tells us that God redeems us from slavery[88], the realm of the dead[89], the pit[90], our offenses[91], the curse of law[92], and from *all* wickedness (emphasis mine).[93] The obvious implication is that we were slaves, dead, in the pit, offensive, cursed by law keeping, and wicked. Show me one self-sufficient, perfectly competent attribute in all of that. Without all of this mess, there would be no redemption, no Redeemer. All that came before no longer holds us captive because of the purchase out of slavery, mistakes, shame, and regrets. It isn't that the past doesn't matter. Rather, the past has now become a vehicle for our Redeemer to exchange our slavery for freedom, our shame for dignity, our sin for purity: beauty instead of ashes, gladness instead of mourning, praise instead of a spirit of despair.[94]

The shocking beauty is that nothing ugly: no pain, disease, violence, despair, or anguish, is wasted on a God who takes all the cast-off ugliness we want to forget, and turns it into something that blesses us beyond what our minds can comprehend. He doesn't see what is ugly for anything other than a grand excuse to buy us back. The God of the universe will find any and all reasons to bring us back to himself, to restore us, to reconcile us, to redeem us. He has chosen, out of his great heart of love, to employ every means possible to bring us to himself. All of us. Even the people you may love to hate.

This redemption is unfair, nothing we earn. We don't look pretty in our realm-of-the-dead apparel, offensive and wicked. And neither do those we hate the thought of forgiving for their realm-of-the-dead outfits. The fact is, our Redeemer redeems us out of the curse of law-keeping. How is that for unfair treatment of law-abiding citizens who want to get all gussied up in Sunday dress and impress God? He calls it cursed.

Without our brokenness and bondage, we have no need of redemption. Make note again of the list of things we're redeemed from, not only our own doing, but also what has been done to us. It is because of where we've been that we have a Redeemer. He gives great meaning and value to the moments, days, and years we may feel were wasted, by using them to bring us his great gift of redemption. We cannot provide it for ourselves. Years of waste and the ensuing regrets are the signposts guiding us to our redemption. Our Redeemer takes the waste and turns it into something that grows us, moves us along on his journey, un-sticks us from our stuck places and then shows us how being stuck prepared us for the good that he could bring out of it. Dates and time don't return to us, and lost opportunities have left, but the waste becomes fertile ground in which redemption can take hold. We grow, our loved ones grow, love grows, endurance and patience grow, forgiveness becomes possible, and regrets are released to redemption. We are the Redeemed.

REDEEMED

Naming ourselves the Redeemed frees us to drop all the former thought patterns that have ensnared us in a life of ever-deepening bleakness. We learn, gradually, how to nurture gratitude for the redemption that is ours, in spite of the reality of our circumstances. Instead of the negativity that a Victim must cultivate, the Redeemed, when faced with the truth of what has been done for them, begin the long process out of old names with the natural response of gratitude—gratitude for grace. And grace received means grace can now be freely given.

Though the research on rats and humans that Sapolsky described indicates a biological predisposition to respond a certain way to lack of control and unpredictability, this does not define what our response to these must be. Lack of predictability and control are a product of design. The human mind has limitations. It was designed by God to be incapable of seeing into the future, to be limited in knowledge to only experience, learning, and the all-subjective (therefore flawed) interpretations of both. Our minds, though having great capacity, were also designed to have limited capacity. Rescuers and Victims both would alter their courses if they could acknowledge that these two "missing pieces" in their capability are actually valued by God, evidenced in the fact that this is exactly how we are designed—without the capability for total predictability and control. In the mysterious wisdom of God, he wants us to face unpredictability and lack of control in life. Rather than responding like rats to unpredictability and loss of control, we have the capacity to expect both as God's design.

I'm not suggesting we have to enjoy this reality, but I do believe a wise (and peaceful) response is to accept it with thanksgiving rather than hopelessness and despair. Writing from God's perspective, Sarah Young pens in her devotional *Jesus Calling*, "Welcome challenging times as opportunities to trust Me"[95], and "Anticipate coming face to face with impossibilities: situations totally beyond your ability to handle."[96] Throughout this devotional, which seems to me ideally suited for anxious struggles, Young recounts her own learnings from God as she has prayed and meditated on his word. She crafts these into a highly accessible and biblical form, focusing on the path of peace, rather than the trails we often find ourselves on, particularly as we are faced with adversity.

This devotional reflects Young's understanding that God asks us to view the unpredictable and inevitable hardships of life with anticipation, expectation, trust and thankfulness. Our hope is in the intentionality of a Redeemer who has a plan to bring good out of the rubble.

Isaiah 44:22 challenges a Victim to live the truth of who they really are. "I have swept away your offenses like a cloud, your sins like the morning mist. Return to me, for I have redeemed you." Redemption is ours for the taking, but sometimes we are so foolish, we prefer to live in slavery. Our Redeemer tells us to return to him because the purchase out of slavery has already been made. Regardless of what we call ourselves, we're already Redeemed. Are you still languishing in a puddle on the floor of your prison? Why not unclench your hand and take out the key that has always been yours, opening the door to redemption? We are not Victims. That is not our name. It may have been a state we were in, or may even be a state we again find ourselves in, but it is not who we are and it will not overcome us if we return to him and let him make redemption our reality, in his time and his way.

We don't need approval. He's already given it. We don't need to complain that life is unfair. In the unfairness lies our redemption. We don't need to manipulate and control people so we can cling to them. We are never alone, even when we're faced with the possibility of rejection. Isaiah again points us in the right direction. "Fear not, for I have redeemed you; I have summoned you by name; you are mine. When you pass through the waters I will be with you; and when you pass though the rivers, they will not sweep over you. When you walk through the fire, you will not be burned; the flames will not set you ablaze."[97] And Jesus reiterated "In this world you will have trouble. But take heart. I have overcome the world."[98] We are not a mere number in God's billions of people here on earth. We belong to the Redeemer and he calls us by name.

I was deeply moved by a story I was told when I visited Cambodia. The woman telling it was someone who had spent a good deal of her adult life ministering in Cambodian prisons. That in itself was amazing to me, having just returned from Phnom Penh's military hospital, which seemed more a prison than a place of healing. I couldn't imagine what prison must look like. That hospital had only touched the surface of suffering in this country of gently spoken, industrious, largely young people with few elders.

The woman told us of a man from China who she found naked in his own bodily fluids, lying motionless on the prison floor, a small washcloth his only source of privacy. He was in the final stages of AIDS. No one cared and no one attended him. He could not move to address any of his needs, so there he lay, waiting to die. She wasted no time finding an interpreter and telling him of God's love for him, no matter what had brought him to prison or what regrets he had. His past couldn't hold him back from the rich love of God, and as she spoke, he told her he remembered, there in that place of dank despair, a story of hope he heard of Christ as a child. He grasped onto the gift of redemption that day, and shortly thereafter died in a joy she watched transform him even in his lifeless body. He died under the care and watch of his Redeemer, as the Redeemed. God had taken all that looked like waste from this man's past and turned it into broken and ugly steps out of darkness into light.

This is the kind of beauty that brings glory to God. He's not looking for our success stories and our comfortable lives to reveal his heart. This is the display of his splendor as he reaches down into our pit and reveals to us just how gracious and powerful his love for us is. He is not the God of credentials, checking to see our accomplishments, our status, and our religious savvy. He is the God of the sick, sinner, poor in spirit, and weak. He delights in redemption. He rejoices when what was lost is found, when the lost past becomes the footing for a redeeming work.

It's a curious thing that we'd prefer to stay stuck with the name Victim, refusing this beautiful redemption. Though destructive to the core, Victim remains a favored name for coping with the problems of life. This idol has been passed down from generation to generation. I Peter 1:18 puts it this way: "For you know that it was not with perishable things such as silver or gold that you were redeemed from the empty way of life handed down to you from your ancestors." This is an admonishment, a reminder, not to return to the empty things that generations of sin have handed down. But we have a problem. We absorb things from our surroundings and they become so deeply ingrained that they are, to us, perfectly legitimate ways to respond, to think and act. We believe we're destined to live under the bondage of the name Victim, even though we're the Redeemed.

Pain, anguish, the ravages of sin against us, abuses, tragedies that befall us—these are all real events to which we fall victim. But, the Redeemer has bought back slaves, grasshoppers, clay pots, and dust that will return to dust, from all they've done or that has been done to them, and has restored them to what he has decided is their proper place of honor. We are powerless, utterly and absolutely, but instead of that driving us to despair, it lifts us up as we rest in the ultimate power of the one whose gift has been ours all along, waiting to be realized.

Anxiety at a Glance

OUR FALSE IDENTITY:

- Victim

DETRIMENTAL THOUGHTS AND BELIEFS:

- Need for control
- Need for approval
- Ascribing blame
- Unhealthy dependencies
- An over-developed sense of justice

BEHAVIORAL EXAMPLES:

- Convincing others of where injustices have been done
- Seeking approval for personal behavior found unacceptable but believed to be unavoidable
- Using means that can potentially drive people away
- Anticipating rejection, certain it is deserved

THE REDEEMER'S IDENTITY FOR US:

- Redeemed

Scriptures for Meditation

Job 19:25, Job 40:8, Psalm 49, Isaiah 40:27-31, Isaiah 43:14-25, Isaiah 57:14-21, Isaiah 61:1-3, Isaiah 65:17-25, Luke 4:18-21, John 12:30-32, Romans 7:7-8:1, Philippians 3:12-14, Philippians 4:8-9, Hebrews 8:8-12, Revelation 21:1-5.

CHAPTER TEN

Pilgrims

W E LIVED IN ENGLAND for a year, and on the May long weekend we took a wonderful trip to the Cotswolds just north and west of London. The area is renowned for its quintessential English countryside, meandering rivers and streams, limestone cottages, and gentle nature full of trees, birds and pasture land.

The day that we decided to take a public footpath between the towns of Lower Slaughter and Upper Slaughter (the name is derived from the Old English name for wetland) was a warm and sunny one. The trip was no more than a mile, but we were there for the journey, not the arrival, and so our walk was unhurried as we took in the restful beauty of our surroundings. On either end of our trip, through the farmer's fields, we passed through livestock gates, intended, it seemed, mostly for sheep because little other livestock is seen on the green, rolling hillsides. Though we'd never been there before, we had no trouble finding the markers for the footpath, Warden's Way, and the path itself was well-worn from the many wayfarers before us. We were pilgrims, journeying in a foreign land, trusting only the small signs pointing to a path and the worn dirt beneath our feet—margins set clearly by pasture growth beside it that had not been trampled. Someone knew the way and we would follow.

Scripture does refer to us as sheep, but I see myself less as a sheep and more a Pilgrim. I had no trouble getting through the gates on either end of the fields we walked across. Sheep aren't capable of doing that. Pilgrims must have their wits about them, must be alert to the dangers on the journey, watch for the signposts along the way, and figure out where to get supper. A Pilgrim is someone who has powers of reasoning, skills of ingenuity, and ways and means of survival a sheep doesn't have. Pilgrims can use their minds to get into all sorts of trouble too, but none-the-less, they can think. Pilgrims know where they want to arrive, but they don't necessarily know the way. Pilgrims need a guide, just as Warden's Way was guided by those who went before. Pilgrims need to have a place of arrival in mind, and a sense of which path to take to get there. Pilgrims need someone trustworthy who knows the way.

On my trip to Cambodia, our group of women stopped overnight in Bangkok. Having been on the streets of Phnom Penh, Bangkok was suddenly a return to the Western World to which I was accustomed. So when I and two other women asked our wonderfully polite doorman at the hotel if he knew where we could get a river tour, we happily jumped into the cab he hailed and let him give the driver instructions. After all, we were surrounded by concrete high-rises.

Our cab driver drove us through the streets of Bangkok, an adventure in itself if you've ever been in traffic in Asia, and we watched through the windows as the city surrounded us with familiar looking structures. Then our driver took a turn down a back road, behind hotels that looked less familiar from the back and into a small cul-de-sac with a thrown together shack just off the river. We were met by a man who had already been alerted by our hotel doorman, and his greeting was the customary graciousness we had been met with throughout our trip. I asked if I could use the restroom, and he pointed to an area for women only, refusing to let me go near where the men went. Looking at the entrance to either location, I decided I didn't really need to use the facilities after all. We were no longer in the comfortable hotel strip.

Our host led us down to the river banks and we were awed at its size, so near the entrance to the Gulf of Thailand. The water was full of silt and it seemed a long way to the other side. We were ready, as we'd been told a river cruise in Bangkok was not to be missed. This was the last of our adventures before returning home. In Cambodia, our group had been shot at, had a near miss accident at high speeds on a crowded highway, and been driven through the traffic filled streets of Phnom Penh on the front of a cyclo (a cycle rickshaw with the bike in behind the passenger), our feet and legs the only crumple zone as we jostled for position with military trucks and vehicles crammed with people. We felt no fear, we three women, on our own in Bangkok.

Approaching the banks was our ride, a truly Thai boat, long and sleek, navigating the waves comfortably. We waited for it to stop and in we got, seating ourselves carefully as the boat rocked in the waves of this vast river, then out to the water we set. Only then did I look for a life jacket. Behind us, lying at the back of the boat, were vests that looked like they had once had the capability of being buoyant, perhaps 30 years earlier. We began to hit waves head-on, which diverted my attention from the lifeless life vests. The planks in the bottom of the boat were actually slapping against each other, as if not quite secured down. These large waves seemed to want to challenge our boat as each onslaught sent a spray of water into our faces. Duly warned about drinking water in Southeast Asia, I licked my lips so they stuck shut, and squinted hard. Nothing was getting in.

My fellow travelers spoke to me as we crossed the breadth of the river, to which I only responded with a squinty nod or shake of the head. I wasn't taking any chances. After all I'd seen on this trip full of adventure, it was the microscopic creatures that unnerved me. Still, the trip was wonderful and gave us a lovely perspective of the city, and then we finally arrived at the other side of the river, out of the waves and I opened my eyes fully to take in the sights.

We entered a canal off the river, and with it, another world. Suddenly, we were in the reality of many of the people of Bangkok. Central Bangkok, with its Western structures, had somehow lulled me into forgetting where I was. The poverty was clear, and once again I found myself in a foreign land. It occurred to me now that we were three foreigners led by a man we did not know even the name of, recommended to us by another man we did not know. I was suddenly very aware that we might not be as smart the adventurers that we'd thought we were. I sat in this boat, in a beautiful country with amazing scenery, and pondered my fate. Who was our hotel doorman anyway? We just jumped in the cab without telling anyone in our party what we were about to do— three North American women, so very much alone. I thought of my family, how they would handle the news that I was missing, with no idea where I might be.

After an agonizing trip through what was a wonderful adventure completely lost on me, we re-entered the river and I resumed my tight-mouthed, squinty-eyed, now relieved posture as tourist in Bangkok, led by a man who turned out to be an entirely trustworthy guide, albeit unprepared for a capsize. I was a tourist now educated about how foolish the idea that she could save herself from parasites in the water, when she hadn't even done a basic safety move like tell someone where she was going. When in new circumstances, which life regularly presents, a Pilgrim maybe isn't as dumb as sheep, but she's still dumb.

A Pilgrim is on a long journey of sacred devotion, headed to a destination in faith that the destination will be there. A Pilgrim is unsure of the terrain ahead and also unsure of the best roads and the dangers inherent along the path. Pilgrims cannot know in advance the heights of ecstasy when summits are reached and the valley views stun the senses. Nor can they avoid the depths of anguish once they inevitably must traverse those same valleys full of hurdles, dark forest floors, and the wild. We've set our hearts on pilgrimage (Psalm 84). We've decided that the city of God is our destination. But where is it, and how do we get there? We can't know what that journey will hold for us and we don't know the way. We need a Shepherd.

We who have set our hearts on pilgrimage are on this unknown journey together, with help from the ancients who trekked before us and fell into plenty of snares, reminders of the necessity to "Trust in the Lord with all your heart and *lean not on your own understanding*."[99] (emphasis mine)

As Pilgrims we make many choices on the journey, and the choices are good and bad, safe and dangerous, brave and fearful, sinful and saintly. It would be lovely to always make great choices, but it isn't realistic, nor is it what God expects of us as he shepherds us.

SHEPHERD

The name shepherd is a bit mystifying for a modern North American, unlike our scriptural ancestors who were very familiar with the nomadic wilderness experience. A shepherd was the leader of a flock for the benefit and protection of that flock. Shepherds needed to have courage, living out a dangerous existence in the wild with any number of predators waiting to pounce on the unsuspecting and helpless sheep. King David's first career was shepherding, and he trusted in God, who had helped him subdue lions and bears, when he seemingly fearlessly went up against the giant Goliath. Shepherding is no job for the timid. It carries a heavy weight of responsibility and leadership, so heavy that scripture applies this name to leadership for God's people.

As often as shepherd is used in scripture to refer to good leadership, it also refers to bad. Bad shepherding is when the shepherd abandons the helpless or misuses power over them. Good shepherds, by contrast, don't leave, and they ensure the flock stays on the right course. Scripture refers to God as the Shepherd, the Rock of Israel[100], and the Shepherd of Israel.[101] Psalm 23, perhaps the most famous reference to this name, says "The Lord is my

Shepherd", and Isaiah says "He tends his flock like a shepherd…
and carries them close to his heart."[102]

God's role as our Shepherd is in stark contrast to some leaders
of Israel who were chastised for poor and misleading shepherding,
when tenderness and care were not their sole priority. When
Christ referred to himself as the "good shepherd", he said the good
shepherd "lays down his life for the sheep."[103] Our Shepherd is full
of tenderness, commitment, and sacrifice as he leads us.

On occasion, while traveling through the cattle country of
Southern Alberta, I've had the opportunity to see a cattle drive.
Though not a common sight, there have been times when I've
seen men or women on horseback riding behind and beside the
herd, trying to contain them on a certain trajectory. Whips are
employed, not to hit the cattle, but to sting the ground beside
them, turning them in fear back to the path necessary for the
journey. Some farmers use dogs to help in this containment and
it always appears there is a necessary element of fear forced on
the cattle to keep them going in the direction they need to head.
I liken that to fire and brimstone preachers who come to the
flock and berate them into submission with fear. They have a
destination in mind, I've no doubt they really care about getting
the flock to the destination, and all fear necessary to keep them
on track is worthy of the end.

Driving with fear is such a divergence from John 10:3a-4: "He
calls his own sheep by name and leads them out. When he has
brought out all his own, he goes on ahead of them, and his sheep
follow him because they know his voice." John Eldredge wrote
something that made this passage very dear to me:

> "I love this passage and have spent a good
> deal of time here. But today I'm struck by
> the phrase "he goes on ahead of them."
> It's almost as if I'd never noticed it before,
> never given it my heart's attention. Jesus
> goes on ahead of us. That is so reassuring,

and that is *such* a different view than the
one with which I approach each day."[104]

Our Shepherd leads by example, by getting out ahead of us
and taking the path he knows well, has traveled before, and is
most committed to guiding us through. Again, though, he is ever
the gentleman, leading with tenderness rather than threats. He
carries us "close to his heart." Our well-being (defined by him and
only understood by him as our Creator) is his first priority, so the
journey is just as important to him as the destination.

Our Shepherd is willing to patiently wait for us to get so
frustrated, tired, and discouraged with our old names, that we'll
abandon them to be lead into his reality. He knows the way
because it's his path, his design and his choice. We need to do just
what John 10 tells us. We need to get in behind him and follow.

What following has meant for me is that I lay down the
research, the heavy lifting of knowing all my options and the
anxiety of knowing exactly what my next move should be. I
shun the "what would Jesus do" notion because the reality is I
DO NOT KNOW what Jesus would do with all the issues that
face me. He didn't give a checklist or textbook for how to live
in every situation. He said "follow me." It is an active, dynamic,
daily decision to not know where you're going and trust that if
you get in behind him, he'll be out in front leading as you start
walking.

His word is a "lamp to our feet and a light to our path."[105]
Imagine yourself on a dark path. The light at your feet leads you,
at best, just a few feet ahead. It doesn't provide a light beam cast
way out ahead so that you can decide what you'll do next. The
life of a Pilgrim is one of complete trust because we are vulnerable
and frail. The life of a Self-sufficient, Perfectly Competent Rescuer
is a life of taking charge of that which is outside of human grasp,
fearfully trying to manage the journey. I've taken both trips, and
I much prefer the peace of the former.

The journey out of old names isn't easy. We've owned them
for too long and have convinced ourselves, not only that we need

them, but that we are obliged to them. We need a Shepherd who knows the way out of the rabbit trail in the thickets that we've got ourselves stuck in. Some of those thickets need a machete, and it will be painful. We may, along with Diane, feel as if body parts are being severed, but our Shepherd is trustworthy and he has set his sights on our freedom and release.[106] Those old names have kept us in bondage and slavery long enough.

Though the Israelites witnessed remarkable miracles in the plagues and the parting of the Red Sea, they still longed to return to their oppression because it was all they knew. They'd been in Egypt for over 400 years! Is it any wonder we, without experiencing the miracles they did, long to return to the slavery of our names that keep us oppressed? It is a prison we create for ourselves because we are too afraid of what freedom might mean.

There are risks involved with any freedom. The freedom to choose to set our sights only on our Shepherd's lead puts all the things we've tried to control at risk. But he offers us a freedom that comes from his knowledge of our best interest, not our best guess for how to run the world. He offers his deep abiding love that sees us as treasures, valued for the worth he has placed on us, not what we've tried so hard to earn for ourselves. Israel's own Pilgrim trek has warned us of the danger of returning to our slavery, ensnared by idols and forgetting who names us.

Our Shepherd loves us, and this love is unfazed by our folly. When we are most broken and most off track is when he is most deeply at work in our lives, moving in ways unseen to bring us onto the path of his peace. Hebrews 11 gives us a view of what real Pilgrims look like. They even get high billing as heroes of faith, yet look at the mess they made in life. This is no list of Pilgrims with flawless execution. Rather, we find ourselves reading messy stories of people who made some hopelessly foolish choices, but were commended for getting in behind God when he told them to. Take a wander through the pages of Judges where you'll find some of the men listed in Hebrews 11, or read David's stories in Samuel, Chronicles and Kings. There was a lot of muddle and poor decision-making in the lives of these heroes of the faith. Judge them by your own standards and you'll condemn them for hideous behavior, but they were commended because of faith— simple sheep-like trust when God asked them to do something. They believed that life lived on the path behind God was bigger than any human frailty that they could apply to a path lived charging ahead of him or running for the nearest hiding place.

It is worth drawing attention to the mess in these men's lives because God doesn't back away from our messy stories. We may, in our attempt to manage God's PR in the world, prefer to rationalize and explain away the bad stuff God appears to ignore. Yet in all of our ugly mire, his main concern seems to be faith, trust and obedience.

> "As the rain and the snow come down
> from heaven, and do not return to it
> without watering the earth and making
> it bud and flourish, so that it yields seed
> for the sower and bread for the eater, so is
> my word that goes out from my mouth:
> It will not return to me empty, but will
> accomplish what I desire and achieve the
> purpose for which I sent it."[107]

He gives us his word, including all these ungainly and cumbersome stories of blemish. These stories invite us to pilgrimage. These stories of flawed men who make seemingly, if not obviously, poor decisions, are stories of the faithful. We are the faithful: the flawed, foolish, embarrassing, and sinful faithful. We are those who give our lives to follow in faith regardless of the state we find ourselves in. We become part of the list in Hebrew 11, not because of things we do or earn, but because he has chosen to bestow grace on those who take this journey in all their weakness.

Competency and sufficiency, good behavior and righteous attempts at keeping laws don't impress the Shepherd. He invites us to accept our failure and just follow his lead. When we're anxious people, we're so busy trying to prove we deserve an "A" that we've entirely missed the point of the pilgrimage. But the path of success that leads to anxiety is easier than the path which accepts our weakness and leads to peace, because the first path woos our love of achievement and glory.

Pilgrims are in this together. We not only need a Shepherd, but we need to be a part of the flock. We were designed to travel in community. We need each other when the mud gets deep and the lures away from the path get unbearably strong. There is no time to attack each other for flaws. The journey is tough enough with attacks from our dangerous surroundings, threatening at any moment to pull us off the well-worn path. We can't be savaging each other, demanding of each other what the Shepherd has not. Faith is what is commended. Pilgrims need to have a lot of faith in the midst of their many doubts, but they don't need to be wonderful, insightful, whole, pleasant, or doctrinally "correct" to make the journey.

Our Shepherd leads us to the streams of grace. These streams flow out from the very throne of God, quenching the thirst of all those who drink. God provides these streams to replenish his Pilgrims. These quenching waters demand a lot of us because we have to share them with a whole bunch of people we find particularly obnoxious.

Sometimes it's hard to accept that God's grace is sufficient for everyone. But Jesus was deliberate. The Shepherd sought the downcast, those sinners who the righteous shunned. He said that those who were forgiven much loved much.[108] He knew our hearts would turn us away in one of two ways. Either we would consider ourselves unworthy or we would consider ourselves worthy indeed. Both paths miss the streams. Both paths look for merit. Grace is meritless, and so those who have no merit to offer are the only ones who can receive the gift.

This pilgrimage is slow, steady and enduring, with change in us often indiscernible to the human eye. The work carries on silently while we love, work, know tragedy and joy, sin, and experience brokenness. We are Human, Transformed, Saved,

Redeemed, the Children of God, even as the pilgrimage leads us in the process of transition into those names.

Just as the moon cannot choose to reflect the light of the sun, we cannot choose to reflect the glory of God. It reflects off of us because he is here, present in our lives and flowing from us. Grace grabs a hold of us in the deepest part of our own human floundering and we are profoundly changed. Life in the realization of grace nurtures in us a deep longing to obey God, serve him, and be faithful, all held in human "jars of clay"[109], that still have holes and cracks. Grace teaches us that our life is not our own. This grace is not life lived in liberty to do as we please. It is a grace to compel us to live life as he meant it to be. The good news of the Gospel is this—God is with us. God is with you: near to you right now wherever you are, whatever your state of mind or heart. He will not leave you. You did not earn his presence and you cannot drive it away. This is the relentless pursuit of God who teaches us how to stop living a religious life, in exchange for living a life of faithful pilgrimage in patient expectation of what he will do with our inability to earn what only he can give.

There is no refuge or safety apart from the dangerous life he calls us to live. We can't do this life our way, masters of our own destiny, controlling outcomes that make us feel safe and secure, and at the same time experience true freedom. This life of peace is the ultimate paradox. If you lose your life, you will save it. Our Shepherd taught us that the secret to life lies in complete abandonment of it, in exchange for a single focus—following his Sovereign lead.

PART THREE

A Story Revisited

CHAPTER ELEVEN

Our Exodus Moment

I WANT TO NEVER again experience anxiety. I wish it would leave me forever, but still it comes on occasion: that familiar old feeling of total immobilization, starving me of an appetite for anything but to run from my own skin. But God doesn't rip it out, destroying it with fire from heaven. Instead, he asks me to walk through it with him; he asks me to remember his name, remember my name, and to look to him for strength. I continue to be a weak vessel through which the work of God is made manifest. If I no longer suffer panic attacks on a regular basis, it isn't because I've figured out the solution and applied it to my life in a formulaic way. It is because of the work of God in my life, the work that happens when I run to him when I'm struggling, when I choose to identify myself according to who he tells me I am. I don't have to be perfect, anxiety-free, or all put together like I would prefer to be. I need to be dependent on a personal God who names me his own, who promises to hold me fast, and who delights in my weakness when I run with it to him.

Have you, like me, cried out to God, begging that he would take your anxiety and panic away? Paul had a similar prayer.

> "There was given me a thorn in my flesh, a messenger of Satan, to torment me (sound familiar?). Three times I pleaded with the Lord to take it away from me. But he said to me, "My grace is sufficient for you, for my power is made perfect in weakness."

Therefore I will boast all the more gladly about my weaknesses, so that Christ's power may rest on me."[110]

So I am boasting to you about my weakness. I'm still someone who has a genetic or nurtured wiring toward a tendency to be anxious. The experts haven't come up with a definitive cause, but even if they one day do, genetics and nurturing will still prevail. Anxiety has long been with the human race, to greater and lesser extents, and if it's my weakness today, it may still be my weakness when I'm 80. So does that mean God just leaves me to my own devices, telling me to just suck it up? No, he says "My grace is sufficient for you."

I said early in the book that acceptance of grace is a barrier to the healing power of God offered to those of us who suffer with this problem of anxiety. For me, this was because I wanted to overcome my problem myself. I wanted to be competent and capable at thinking my way to a solution. I didn't want to accept myself as one who had a weakness, one who needed to wait for God to act. I wanted to do the acting to alleviate the problem, and then take credit for doing just that. I'd much prefer to write a book entitled *How I Conquered Anxiety by Sheer Determination, and You Can Too*. But that isn't how the story of my life goes. Instead, I've learned that help is God's gift to me given in my utter weakness, and I'm named according to that exact weakness. If you can do it on your own you don't need to be redeemed or saved. That's for the weak. A do-it-yourselfer would call you a sissy if you even suggested you were a dependent child. We are named because of our broken humanity, a humanity God entirely understands and has provided his own remedy for, which is his grace, his unearned merit which gives us access to this power only he wields, in his way, on his own time.

Those moments when I beg God to just rip anxiety from me are the same moments that reveal to me the truth about who I am and who he is. They are the moments that help me to see I've gotten myself lost again, lost in the crazy thoughts that get me into trouble in the first place. Those are the crazy thoughts that tell me I need to solve problems alone, that my efforts can somehow thwart the forces of life outside of my control, that the world will stop spinning if I don't execute a decision flawlessly, or that God will punish me somehow if I fail to find that one right answer. He lets anxiety, my great weakness, be my teacher. It's been a steep learning curve.

By no means is the journey out of debilitating anxiety about a journey into thoughtlessness and abandon of human logic. I've taken the time to delineate my own thought processes that were heavily influenced by my relationship with God as he began to transform me. We've been given fine human minds for a reason. We've been given the capacity to grasp thoughts and concepts of great complexity, to use logic and reason and to problem solve. All of these things are at our disposal and we are responsible to use them well. Otherwise, you'd be wasting your time reading this book and I'd be wasting mine writing it. At the same time, we need to consider the reality that as fine as our human minds may be, there is a Mind that is profoundly wise. The profoundness of this wisdom escapes any human understanding that we try to apply to it and this is because we have limitations. God has none, and tells us it is precisely within our limitations that he wishes to reach in and develop in us a life-long relationship of dependency on him.

In no way have I intended for this summary of thought processes and mistakes I've made to become a structured plan for how to fix anxiety. This would be a complete missing of the point, but entirely something an anxious person would want to use it for. Instead, my hope is this will be a provocation to re-think how we approach life. This book is about using the strength of our mind to acknowledge our weakness. The insistence on running our own show out of our strength is exactly what got us in this mess in the first place and it's not going to be the path out. I don't wake up every morning and say, "I know my names and God's names and today I will live without anxiety because I've finally got the formula figured out." In fact, I live everyday dependent on God to transcend the limitations of my intellect by the renewing of my mind[111], because of the power of his Spirit.[112] Can you, an anxious person, even imagine this? I don't do anything other than ask for help when I need it. I just wait, and I acknowledge that I'm powerless to stop my rapidly beating heart and crawling skin. The biggest miracle of all for me is that in my weakness, when I'm most vulnerable and out of control, is when he is able to do this work that transforms me. It's as simple and as difficult as letting go of the reins.

And what of names? How do they change us? It's all in the name. Is God our Punisher or Sacrificial Shepherd? Is he our Task Master or a Gracious Redeemer when failure besets us? Names! Have they become our idols, snares that engulf us and pull us away from God's intent for us? Or have we embraced those names God speaks so often in his word, resting in their significance and mystery. Whatever names we choose, they shape us. God calls us to be shaped in a relationship with him and the names he calls us. We are powerfully and mysteriously shaped into Human by Yahweh, Transformed by the Spirit, a Child of God by our Father, Saved by our Savior, Redeemed by our Redeemer, and Pilgrims lead by our Shepherd.

I've been shaped by my names, shaped into someone who knows peace where I struggled to find it before. When I feel that old surge of cortisol and adrenaline coursing through my veins, I stop and ask God to reveal to me the "rock and the hard place" I've once again managed to wedge myself into. This wisdom I ask for, not to change what I'm doing, but so I can confess, speak his truth about it, and in so doing express my need of his work in my heart to change that way of thinking. And there, humbled again by this weak tendency, I ask that he transform me because my weakness reveals again how wholly dependent I am. I need to be saved from my inclinations, and I am relieved to know even in this moment of weakness, he'll redeem it all.

When we take the time to consider how God gives us a new identity through the names he gives to us, we can no longer look back on our lives as barren wastelands of regret and loss, unrealized dreams and futility, or as evidence of how amazingly skilled at life we are. All of it, every moment we've been given until this moment right now, are the moments our Redeemer counts as necessary for his great work of redemption in us. We may cringe at the thought of some memories, or brag about others, but God cringes at nothing and refuses to let us boast. He will bring about his plans and his names in his time and his way, in spite of and because of all that came before. Nothing is wasted in him.

Have you ever had an Exodus Moment, that moment in your life where God showed you a way out of slavery and bondage? I did. It happened that night on the couch when he told me I was a blade of grass. That night, God invited me to accept weakness and failure as a real portion of our humanity, and to embrace the truth that Sovereign grace was sufficient for all the futility of my efforts. This can in no way become a slumped, defeated, self-hating posture. Instead, it is the recognition that grace is not attainable until we have allowed for the reality and freedom to accept failure. We are all in need of being renewed and renamed, and I'm still growing into my names by the power of God at work in my life. I try to grab back the reins on occasion, probably more than I'd like to admit, but the enduring and persistent work of grace is unyielding. Knowing this, I have asked him to help me yield to it in spite of my preference for calling the shots.

Lord, may your many names be exalted to their rightful place. I love you for your perseverance with me. You are Faithful and True. You've given me a new name I will one day know and that you are preparing me to wear. You are "I AM WHO I AM." Unchangeable. Ineffable. I love that! You challenge me with the words "Who is this that darkens my counsel with words without knowledge?"[113] Who can talk like that? No one is your equal. You have broken me and permitted some of my worst fears to come true, and in all of that, shown me how deep and how wide your love is for me. I love you because nothing in me deserves your love and nothing in me can drive it away. You are who you name yourself, and I am yours. Amen.

Bibliography

BOOKS

Bailey, Kenneth E. *Poet and Peasant and Through Peasant Eyes Combined Edition.* Grand Rapids, MI: Wm. B. Eerdmans, 1983.

Chambers, Oswald. *My Utmost for His Highest.* Grand Rapids, MI: Discovery House, 1935.

Eldredge, John. *Walking With God.* Nashville, TN: Thomas Nelson, 2008.

Griffin, Emilie. *Clinging-The Experience of Prayer.* New York: Harper and Row, 1984 as quoted in Benson, Bob and Benson, Michael W. *Disciplines for the Inner Life.* Nashville, TN: Thomas Nelson, 1989.

Guyon, Jeanne as quoted in Edward, Gene. *100 Days in the Secret Place.* Shippensburg, PA: Destiny Image, 2001.

Peterson, Eugene. *Tell It Slant.* Grand Rapids, MI: Wm. B. Eerdmans, 2008.

Pfeiffer, Charles, ed. and Harrison, Everett F, ed. *Wycliffe Bible Commentary.* Chicago, IL: Moody Press, 1990.

Rahner, Karl. *Encounters with Silence.* Christian Classics, 1984 as quoted in Benson, Bob and Benson, Michael W. *Disciplines for the Inner Life.* Nashville, TN: Thomas Nelson, 1989.

Sapolsky, Robert. *Why Zebras Don't Get Ulcers, 3rd Ed.* New York: St. Martin's Press, 2004

Tozer, A.W. *The Knowledge of the Holy.* New York: Harper and Row, 1975.

Underhill, Evelyn. *Concerning the Inner Life with The House of the Soul.* Eugene, OR: Wipf and Stock, 2004.

Wright, N.T. *Simply Jesus.* New York: Harper Collins, 2011.

Young, Sarah. *Jesus Calling.* Nashville, TN: Thomas Nelson, 2004.

Other

Lee, Stan. *Amazing Fantasy #15*: Marvel Comics, 1962.

Osborne, Robert. *August 21, 2011 Sermon*. The Chris Wiersma Podcast, Westside-King'sChurch, http://www.wkc.org/weekends/podcast/podcast.xml

Notes

1. Luke 11:24-26.
2. Psalm 139:23-24a.
3. Emilie Griffin, *Clinging—The Experience of Prayer* (Harper and Row, 1984), quoted in Benson and Benson, *Disciplines for the Inner Life* (Thomas Nelson, 1989), 24-25.
4. Matthew 5:3a.
5. Oswald Chambers, *My Utmost for His Highest* (Discovery House Publishers, 1935, 7/21.
6. Genesis 32:28.
7. Genesis 17:5.
8. Matthew 16:18.
9. Job 9:23-24.
10. Job 31:23.
11. Eugene Peterson, *Tell It Slant* (Wm. E Eerdmans Publishing Co., 2008), 106-107.
12. N.T. Wright, *Simply Jesus* (Harper Collins, 2011), 201.
13. Ibid, 203.
14. A.W. Tozer, The *Knowledge of the Holy* (Harper and Row, 1975), 104.
15. Isaiah 42:8.
16. Hebrews 4:12-14.
17. Peterson, 186.
18. Roman 8:15-16.
19. Psalm 51:16-18.
20. Isaiah 57:15.
21. Isaiah 43:7.
22. Matthew 6:9.

23. Charles F.Pfeiffer, ed., Everett F. Harrison, ed., *Wycliffe Bible Commentary* (Moody Press, 1990), 54-55.

24. Exodus 33:18-23.

25. Jeremiah 17:5.

26. Isaiah 40:7, 22-24.

27. Matthew 23:8-12, Luke 14:7-11.

28. Philippians 2:6.

29. Kenneth E. Bailey, *Poet and Peasant and Through Peasant Eyes* (Wm. B. Eerdmans Publishing Co., 1983), 183.

30. 1 Peter 5:5a-7.

31. Romans 5:8.

32. Robert Osborne, *The Chris Wiersma Podcast: Westside-King'sChurch,* podcast audio, August 21, 2011, http://www.wkc.org/weekends/podcast/podcast.xml.

33. James 2:26.

34. Matthew 5:48.

35. Luke 15:11-32.

36. 1 Corinthians 6:19.

37. 1 Samuel 10:6.

38. Isaiah 40:13.

39. Matthew 10:20, Luke 12:12, John 16:13, Acts 6:3.

40. Exodus 31:3, Isaiah 11:2, Mark 13:11.

41. Psalm 139:7.

42. Isaiah 59:21.

43. 2 Corinthians 3:6.

44. 2 Corinthians 3:17.

45. Romans 8:26, Ephesians 3:16.

46. Psalm 139:7 and 23-24.

47. I Kings 19:12.

48. Karl Rahner, *Encounters with Silence* (Christian Classics, 1984), quoted in Benson and Benson, *Disciplines for the Inner Life* (Thomas Nelson, 1989), 304.

49. Proverbs 3:5-6.

50. Psalm 91:1.

51. Jeanne Guyon, quoted in Gene Edwards, *100 Days in the Secret Place* (Destiny Image Publisher, 2001), 50.

52. Matthew 5:48.

53. Mark 10:25.

54. Luke 6:28-30.

55. Matthew 5:44.

56. Stan Lee, *Amazing Fantasy #15* (August 1962).

57. Matthew 5:48.

58. Luke 6:27-36.

59. Matthew 6:8.

60. Matthew 18:10.

61. Matthew 6:25-26.

62. John 10:28.

63. Matthew 18:12-14.

64. Luke 12:32.

65. Psalm 139:10.

66. Bailey, 164.

67. Matthew 6:33.

68. Matthew 6:27.

69. Evelyn Underhill, *Concerning The Inner Life with The House of the Soul* (Wipf and Stock Publisher, 2004), 92.

70. John 10:29.

71. Psalm 91:2.

72. Matthew 16:24-25.

73. 2 Samuel 22:3.

74. Psalm 51:14.

75. Psalm 68:19.

76. Isaiah 19:20.

77. Isaiah 43:11, Hosea 13:4.

78. Romans 14:11.

79. Genesis 18:18, Deuteronomy 4:6, I Chronicles 16:23-25.

80. Isaiah 52:10.

81. Ps. 46:10.

82. Philippians 2:8.
83. Luke 4:18.
84. Galatians 5:1.
85. Rom. 5:3-4.
86. Robert Sapolsky, *Why Zebras Don't Get Ulcers* (St. Martin's Press, 2004), 301.
87. Ibid, 303.
88. Deuteronomy 7:8.
89. Psalm 49:15.
90. Psalm 103:4.
91. Isaiah 44:22.
92. Galatians 3:13.
93. Titus 2:14.
94. Isaiah 61:3.
95. Sarah Young, *Jesus Calling* (Thomas Nelson, 2004), 6/4.
96. Ibid, 8/18.
97. Isaiah 43:1-2.
98. John 16:33.
99. Proverbs 3:5.
100. Genesis 49:24.
101. Psalm 80:1.
102. Isaiah 40:11.
103. John 10:11.
104. John Eldredge, *Walking with God* (Thomas Nelson, 2008), 45.
105. Ps. 119:105.
106. Isaiah 61.
107. Isaiah 55:10-11.
108. Luke 7:46.
109. 2 Corinthians 4:7.
110. 2 Corinthians 12:8-9.
111. Romans 12:2.
112. Luke 11:13.
113. Job 38:2.

CPSIA information can be obtained at www.ICGtesting.com
Printed in the USA
BVOW02s1102190813

328668BV00013B/4/P